Burpee Basics

bulbs

BURPEE.

Burpee Basics

bulbs

A growing guide for easy, colorful gardens

Douglas Green

Macmillan • USA

MACMILLAN
A Simon & Schuster Macmillan Company
1633 Broadway
New York, NY 10019

Macmillan Publishing books may be purchased for business or sales promotional use.
For information please write: Special Markets Department, Macmillan Publishing USA,
1633 Broadway, New York, NY 10019.

Library of Congress Cataloging-in-Publication Data

Green, Douglas.
    Bulbs : a growing guide for easy, colorful gardens / by Douglas Green.
        p. cm.—(Burpee basics)
    Includes index.
    ISBN: 0-02-862637-0
    1. Bulbs.   I. Title.   II. Series.
SB425.G595   1998   98-31051
635.9'4—dc21   CIP

Manufactured in the United States of America
10 9 8 7 6 5 4 3 2 1

Book design by Nick Anderson

Cover design by Michael Freeland

Cover photograph courtesy W. Atlee Burpee

Photography Credits:
    Charles Cresson: page 129
    International Bloembollen Centrum Hillegom, Holland: pages ii, xvi, 4, 5, 8–9, 24, 44, 49, 51,
        52, 54, 56–60, 62–64, 67–72, 78–82, 88–97, 99, 100, 102, 103, 106, 107, 115, 122, 124,
        127, 130, 132, 140, 141
    Greg Piotrowski: pages 88 ('Princess Irene'), 114

Illustration Credit: Laura M. Robbins

For Eugene and Christina Green, Mom and Dad,
who couldn't teach me gardening so taught me the
important stuff instead.

Burpee Basics: Growing Guides for Easy, Colorful Gardens
Down-to-earth handbooks for beginning gardeners

Available from Macmillan Publishing

Burpee Basics: Annuals, by Emma Sweeney
Burpee Basics: Perennials, by Emma Sweeney
Burpee Basics: Roses, by Mary C. Weaver
Burpee Basics: Bulbs, by Douglas Green

To order a Burpee catalogue:

phone: 800-888-1447
email www.burpee.com

or write:

Atlee Burpee & Co.
300 Park Avenue & Co.
Warminster, PA 18974

Contents

Foreword

Gardeners have been looking to Burpee for basic information about how to garden, and for the seeds and plants to implement their dreams, for almost 125 years. In one or the other of the six different catalogs we publish each year, a gardener can find just about any kind of plant his or her heart desires. Our big annual seed catalog, the *Burpee Annual,* has become a gardening Bible. (If you've never had the pleasure of paging through one, there's information in the front of this book about how to get your own free copy.)

What you hold in your hands—one of our new series of concise gardening guide books—is a continuation of that proud tradition of giving gardeners the essentials that they need. These handy little books have a great deal in common with seeds: Each one contains all you need to start a wonderful gardening experience, one that will grow year by year. Successful gardens are built on a constant reworking of the fundamentals. Even the most experienced gardeners, season after season, attend to the basic practices that you'll find so skillfully explained in these guides.

If you're a novice gardener, *Burpee Basics* will help you quickly find the information you need to get started; those of you who are more seasoned can use the books as invaluable reference tools to remind yourself when to start the marigold seeds or divide the anemones, how to cut back the roses or determine the right amount of fertilizer for daffodils . . . all the details you need to keep your plants at their best.

We've made these books conveniently sized as well as easy on the eyes, hoping they'll find a valued spot not on your coffee table but on the shelf above your potting bench or in your garden workroom, right next to your seed packets, where they'll become as well worn and comfortable in your hand as a favorite trowel or trusty clippers.

George Ball, Jr.

Acknowledgments

A bulb garden is a bit like a book in that both start with an idea or a dream. One starts in the ground, the other in the mind; they continue to grow, sight unseen, for about six months before seeing the light of day.

The major difference is that, while the overwintering bulb garden does most of the work itself without help from the gardener, the author of a book is helped along by many other people. It is to these people that these pages are dedicated.

The resources of the Netherlands Flowerbulb Information Center (both in Toronto and New York City) were freely available to me for this project, and I want to acknowledge their generous assistance. They do their jobs well and keep authors like me on the right road.

I am pleased that the editorial team of Barbara Berger and Gregory Piotrowski Berger managed to make sure the text made sense. Their light but deft touch made the process almost enjoyable.

There are many gardeners who share bulbs, seeds, and advice through plant organizations such as the North American Rock Garden Society and on the Internet via, for example, Alpine-L. My record keeping is not extensive enough to track them all, but each gardener deserves a plant hero award. One in particular, Andrew Osyany, got me started on small bulbs and was kind enough to send me extensive lists of bulbs he thought I should grow. Although this was too many years ago to count, I still have the letter and his kind words, and I'm still working on finding all the bulbs.

I am grateful to my agent, Jeanne Fredericks, who helps me with the business side of writing, injects a note of book business sanity into my day now and then when I need it, and did the initial work for this book.

Special thanks go to my kids at home, Robert and Elizabeth, who did the weeding of the bulb beds while I worked on the word processor. The bulb beds are outside my office window and I had to listen to their music—they didn't complain about my work and I didn't complain about their music. A fair trade.

I am also indebted to the countless listeners on my radio show who ask interesting questions that lead me to discover new ways of looking at gardens and growing bulbs. These folks teach me the questions to ask.

Doug Green

Introduction

Growing bulbs is easy.

Talking about bulbs and tubers and how to plant them, Mrs. Jane Loudon suggested in her classic 1851 book, *Ladies Companion to the Flower Garden*:

> These distinctions, however, though they may be interesting to the botanist and vegetable physiologist, are of little or no use in practice; the practical gardener treating bulbs and tubers exactly alike, and planting them as he would sow a seed: that is to say, he fixes them firmly in the ground and covers them, but not so deeply as they exclude the air.

It was simple then, and it remains so today. Put the bulbs in the ground, wait a few summer weeks or winter months, and then relax and enjoy the show. Most bulbs do not get serious diseases; and once you learn how to protect them from squirrels, your garden will never be the same. I confess that my love for bulbs is evident in my garden and the increasing numbers of bulbs that are found there. In the very early spring, the fritillaries jump up in the rock garden, as do the smaller tulips, species iris, and daffodils. These early bloomers are a delight, because they are almost the first thing to bloom after a hard northern zone 4 winter. By early May, the first tulips in the main borders are poking up, and by mid-May they are in full bloom, giving our perennial border a decidedly sunset pink tone. Far away from the pinks of the tulips are the yellows of the daffodils, flowering quite contentedly in their naturalized positions under trees and around the nursery buildings. These plants often get picked for impromptu bouquets that are given to the love of my life. When the tulips, daffodils, and other spring bulbs fade away, the main perennial border is given over to the initial show of perennials and early roses, accompanied by irises. Then, like magic, along come the lilies with their sweet fragrances and amazing colors—the highlight of the summer garden.

In the cutting garden, the gladiolus are a rainbow of beautiful shades, and the surprisingly hardy galtonia gives us a late-summer surprise with its aromatic white blossoms. And then there are all the tiny bulbs—the scilla, galanthus, crocus, arums, and others—too numerous to mention in a short introduction. These live in various parts of the garden and are given homage later in this book.

Not only are bulbs easy to grow, they are fun as well. Learning only a few tricks to discourage pests and several cultural details to keep the bulbs growing happily, any gardener can appreciate outdoor color from early spring until late fall. Even in the winter, gardeners can force bulbs. We routinely plunge a few pots of tulips under several feet of mulch and dig them out midwinter to enjoy a head start on spring. Year-round bulbs are possible with a minimum of planning and preparation.

Often, visitors to my gardens will ask me, "Where did you get *that* bulb?" I do admit to starting a few of my species lily bulbs from seed; but for the most part, I shop at the same places that you do—at garden centers with a reputation for obtaining interesting bulbs. Sometimes I spend hours searching through catalogs, looking for the unusual form or just the right color to match the other flowers in a particular garden bed. After all, when catalogs such as *The Daffodil Mart* can feature almost a thousand (perhaps more by the time this is printed) types of daffodils alone, almost everybody can find something different from what is being grown by his or her neighbors. Growing bulbs, whether for spring blooms, summer spectacles, or quiet fall moments, is not only easy gardening but great gardening.

the fundamentals for easy bulb gardening

The Essentials

- How to Buy Bulbs
- Bloom Period
- How to Plant
- When to Plant
- Ideas for Designing with Bulbs
- How to Cut Flowers from Your Garden
- Summer and Winter Care of Spring-Flowering Bulbs

If bulbs are really that easy to grow, why do we need a section on the basics of selecting and growing them? You *can* grow bulbs without reading anything; but once you understand how bulbs grow best, subsequent garden performance can be improved and the neighbors' envy levels truly tested.

How to Buy Bulbs

In the fall it seems that everyone is selling bulbs. To ensure that the bulbs fit your garden needs, use the following guidelines when heading off on bulb-purchasing expeditions.

Make a List

The first thing that every gardener should do before going to a local garden center or opening a catalog is to make a shopping list. To save time and money, jot down your choices of when the bulb is to flower, how tall the bloom should be, and the colors required. Then find the bulbs that will meet these requirements. You might not always stick to your choices, but the list will serve as a beginning. Gardeners are suckers for new and unusual plants and pretty colors; and when they see a beautiful picture on the label, the plant simply has to go into the shopping basket. Garden business people know this, and there is a very simple phrase in the industry that says everything you need to know to become a wise consumer: "Color sells." Knowing that those wonderful color pictures exist solely as temptations puts you one step above the rest of the consuming and gardening public.

Read the Labels

Most of the packaging that comes with bulbs includes clear directions about cultural care. It is the same with the vast majority of catalogs; for the different bulbs and their varieties they list height, color, and cultural details (like the depth of planting). Although it is a simple thing, reading the label will provide most of the information necessary for success. One cultural detail that the label will usually provide is the recommended zone for successful cultivation. Gardening zones are climatic areas based on average maximum and minimum temperatures and annual rainfall. The zone can be used as a simple guideline that will tell you which plants will survive the cold and heat of your area. Advanced gardeners may modify their soils or create microclimates so they can grow specialized bulbs, but beginning gardeners should pay attention to the zone recommendations and start with plants that are rated for their area. See the map on page 150 to determine your climatic zone.

Check the Bulb

Unfortunately, you cannot check the bulbs before buying through a mail-order catalog; but when you go to a garden center, follow these general guidelines:

1. Bigger is better. The inescapable fact is that bigger bulbs produce either bigger blooms or more of them. Bargain bulbs are simply smaller or younger versions of those jumbo-sized bulbs we want in our own garden. If you are planting the bulb in a high-traffic area, such as near the front door, then the jumbo bulbs are necessary for a good show. The bargain-basement bulbs are fine, however, for naturalizing an area or for more hidden sections, where they will not be seen in quite so intimate a space. The special deals that are often seen in bargain flyers confirm the old adage: You get what you pay for.
2. Avoid soft, mushy, and moldy bulbs. Sometimes there will be nicks and scars on the bulbs; avoid these bulbs as well, even if it looks as if the bulb had healed.
3. Sometimes the bulb's tunic, the papery covering surrounding the bulb, will be torn or ripped. This is not a disqualification point. The tunic can be torn during shipping; and if the underlying bulb is not soft or bruised, the bulb is fine. A torn tunic is not necessarily a symptom of a poor bulb.

After you've purchased the bulbs that meet your list's criteria, why not experiment? Join the rest of the gardening world and try a half dozen bulbs of something new and different. Let them meet your list's color requirements;

A garden showstopper—giant allium.

but try, for example, a small unfamiliar *Merendera* or a huge giant allium—expand your horizons. Similarly, try a new source every year or two. While sticking to suppliers who have good produce, do try to find a new catalog or two for experimentation purposes. ("Bulb Sources" at the end of this book is a good place to start.) Pick from the new and unusual bulbs these specialty sources often supply. Buy only a few dollars' worth from a new supplier, so you can evaluate their bulbs and service. Writing off a small order with a new company is easier than losing your main or big-dollar order.

Bloom Period

By using different cultivars, it is possible to enjoy tulips for more than 30 days. Traditionally, tulips are allowed to bloom; and then once the leaves have faded, the bulbs are overplanted with annual flowers. Late tulips do not finish their bloom time and leaf fading until summertime; thus it is difficult to plant annuals earlier enough for them to reach a large size. If early tulips are grown, however, overplanting can be done at the beginning of June, or sooner, making for a much better performance from the annuals.

Having written this, I must point out that every spring is different and that a hot, dry spring will finish off the blooms much faster than a cool, wet spring. This is another reason to focus on early-blooming bulbs if you hope to do a lot of fill-in planting. Early bulbs will give you a much better chance of planting a fill-in crop of annuals in a late spring season than will the late-flowering bulbs.

If the other plants in the garden are perennials, then you can install a variety of bulbs with wide range of bloom times. Enjoy the bulbs for their addition to the spring garden; and when the bulb foliage fades, do not be concerned with refilling that spot. The bulb and perennial foliage coexist; and as the bulbs fade, the perennials grow over the bulbs and take their place. Remember that most spring-flowering bulbs demand a few weeks to a month of full sunshine after blooming to allow their leaves to photosynthesize and store energy for the following year's bloom. If they have not gathered this energy because an impatient gardener cut down or tied up their foliage, the next year's blooms will be smaller or nonexistent.

When purchasing bulbs, pick those that are consistent with your garden's color scheme and blooming period to ensure that the colors blend well. In other words, do not put a flaming red late tulip next to an early-blooming pink perennial such as *Pulmonaria montana* 'Red Start'. Try the red tulip next to the rich red summer-blooming *Phlox paniculata* 'Starfire'.

The subtle pinks of Allium christophii *are enhanced by the hotter pink tones of* Geranium psilostemon.

Check the bulb boxes at your garden center or the catalog descriptions to ensure the chosen bulbs are going to bloom in your area when you want them to and will not interfere with the rest of your garden.

How to Plant

It takes a blind leap of faith to plant a small, fleshy bulb into the ground and truly expect it to produce a glorious flower after a long, frozen winter. Planting bulbs is easy; holding on to the dream over winter is the hard part.

Regular Planting

The rule of thumb for planting any bulb is to put it two to three times as deep as the bulb is long. A 2-inch tulip bulb goes 4 to 6 inches down (that's 4 to 6 inches between the soil surface and the top of the bulb); plant a 3-inch-long daffodil bulb 6 inches down. It does not get much simpler than that. As Mrs. Loudon said, quoted in the "Introduction," the gardener "fixes them firmly in the ground and covers them," and that is all there is.

Fixing them firmly does not mean pushing the bulb into the hard soil at the bottom of a hole. Gently place the bulb, normally pointy side up, on the bottom of the hole and cover it with soil. If you are not sure about which end of the bulb is up, relax—the bulb knows, and will come up fine. Once the bulb is situated, a simple backfilling will suffice to finish off the job. Unlike planting annuals or perennials, there is no need to stomp the ground down to ensure the soil is firmly fixed around the roots. Instead, water thoroughly (called *mudding in*) to settle the soil and to try to convince chipmunks and squirrels that there really is not anything worth eating in this mud. (See page 26 for chipmunk and squirrel control tips.)

Some gardening books recommend putting bone meal or other fertilizer into the hole when the bulb is planted. Although bone meal will not generally do any harm, fertilizer can burn bulb roots, and putting it down the hole is not a good gardening practice. See "How to Fertilize Bulbs," on page 14, for information on maintaining bulb health and flowering ability.

Deep Planting

If rodents are digging and eating your bulbs, deep planting is an ideal technique for any size tulip bulb or larger bulb of any kind. *Deep planting* means putting large spring bulbs deeper than is normally recommended. This is done for two reasons: First, deep planting makes it difficult for rodents to dig up the bulbs. In my gardens, tulips are routinely planted 10–12 inches deep so that the ravenous squirrel and chipmunk population will not use them as their winter food source. Second, if the bulbs are planted deeply, the annual and perennial garden beds over top of them can be cultivated and worked without disturbing the bulbs. Plant and then forget the bulbs; they will be

Most bulbs multiply by setting seed. And as any grade-school student will tell you, there is nobody out in the wild to care for that seed, to water it, feed it, or plant it at the right depth. Although nature takes care of the watering and feeding, bulbs actually bury themselves. Specialized fleshy roots of the young bulb grow downward in the spring and shrivel and die in the fall. This shriveling pulls the mass of the small developing bulb deeper into the soil. This process occurs yearly until the bulb has been dragged down to its proper depth. Once this depth has been achieved, the root changes its physical structure to a "proper" root and the bulb begins to bulk up and begin flowering.

Starting bulb seeds is not difficult. In October or April, cut the bottom off a nursery container (any size is fine but an 8-inch-diameter pot is the easiest). Dig a hole and bury this pot to the rim in a partly shady area of your garden, where it will get morning and/or late afternoon and evening sun. Use either the soil from the hole or good-quality potting soil to fill the sunken, bottomless pot. Slowly pour an entire kettle of boiling water over the soil to sterilize it. After the soil has cooled, sprinkle bulb seeds over it, placing them at least $1/2$ inch apart. Cover with $1/8$ inch of potting soil, and keep damp. Seeds may take up to two years to germinate, so be patient.

When the tiny, round, grasslike stalks start to grow, allow them to stay in the carefully weeded pot for their first summer of growth. After the first summer, you can dig the small bulblets from their germinating home and move them to a permanent spot in the garden. Plant the bulblets at the same depth in the garden soil as they were when you dug them out of the nursery container. Alternately, you can allow the bulblets to stay in the pot for the winter and move them when they start to die back after their second year of growth. (I routinely start and plant lily and specialized bulb seeds this way.)

fine on their own. Although tulips are the prime candidates for deep planting, many other large spring bulbs can also be treated this way. A few years ago, I changed the elevation of one of my gardens, which caused some forgotten hyacinth bulbs to be buried 3 feet deep. Although I do not know how long they would have continued to bloom from that depth, they did make a good show for several spring seasons, until I finally destroyed them by preventing the plants from setting leaves. Smaller bulbs, such as crocus, generally do not require deep planting. If they remain undisturbed by rodents during their first year, the bulbs will seldom if ever be eaten or dug up.

Rising Bulbs

Do deep-planted bulbs work their way to the surface?

I have contradictory evidence in my own garden for this. Some deep-planted bulbs in my garden have been in place at 12 to 14 inches deep for approximately eight years. They have not moved up; and I wish they would, because they are a striking red and the garden they are now in has been changed to a soft pink tone. I fished around and found many of them, but every spring I'm reminded that I did not get them all. Other bulbs that were planted two years

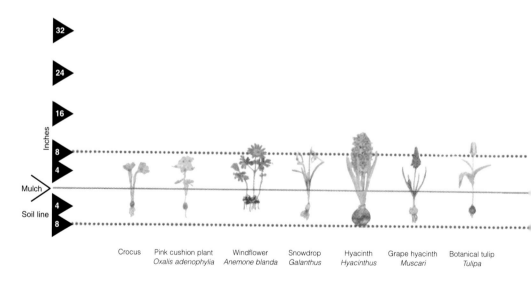

Planting depth chart for various bulbs.

ago at a depth of 8 inches in very shallow soil (9 inches to bedrock) surfaced this year during routine cultivation. It is possible the frost moved them up in much the same way it moves up house-sized boulders in my garden every year (at least they seem house sized). I do know many gardeners who have planted their tulip bulbs 12 inches deep to eliminate rodent problems, and I have not heard any of them report that the bulbs worked their way upward.

How to Prepare the Soil

Preparing the soil for bulbs is much like preparing for almost any other kind of plant. That is to say, when you understand the soil requirements of the bulb to be grown and meet those requirements, then success is only a short wait away. The first thing to understand about bulbs is that they developed their bulbous nature because of the need to store water and food through a

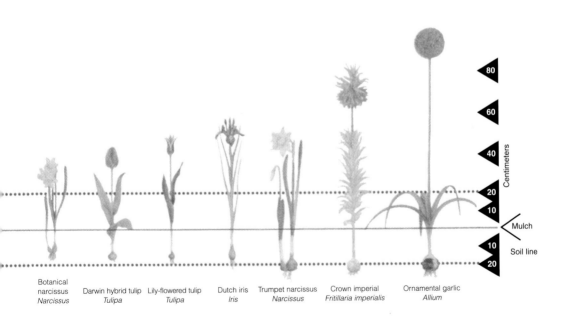

| Botanical narcissus *Narcissus* | Darwin hybrid tulip *Tulipa* | Lily-flowered tulip *Tulipa* | Dutch iris *Iris* | Trumpet narcissus *Narcissus* | Crown imperial *Fritillaria imperialis* | Ornamental garlic *Allium* |

I confess to being a somewhat adventurous gardener (friends might change *adventurous* to *lazy*), and I very often don't follow the advice given in classic gardening manuals. For example, many books recommend planting gladiolus with their root ends down and tell you to be very careful when doing this. For several years, I grew glads commercially and planted well over ten thousand bulbs every year. My main planting device was a tractor and plow. I'd plow a furrow; then walk along it with a large bag full of gladiolus bulbs, throwing them into the plowed trench. They landed in all orientations from the properly upright to the horticulturally depraved upside down.

The next step was to turn the tractor around and plow in the other direction throwing the dirt back onto the trenched glads. This was not what you'd call precision planting; but somehow the glads seemed to know which direction was up, and I never did see any roots, instead of flower stalks, growing out of the ground. Similarly, when I plant my tulips or other bulbs, I use an auger on the end of my electric drill. The auger digs a nice hole about 2 inches across and up to 10 inches deep. When I drop the bulb into the hole, I can assure you I don't check to see if it has landed with the root side down although I do try to properly orient the bulb when before it goes into the hole. Why tempt fate if you don't have to.

Having said that, it is quite probable that bulbs will grow better if they are properly oriented and the roots are indeed placed in the direction that Mother Nature intended. A careful and methodical approach to planting and covering will likely pay dividends, even if only in gardener satisfaction with a job well and properly done. The message here is that, although bulbs may appreciate being oriented in the correct direction, it may not be necessary to be too compulsive about it.

long dry spell. Spring-flowering bulbs are genetically adapted to dry summers, and summer-flowering bulbs are acclimatized to dry winters. Although this is a rule of thumb, sure to be broken by an exception or two, it does tell us something about preparing the soil for bulbs.

The first thing it tells us is that planting bulbs in areas that have standing water for several weeks in any season is a quick recipe for disaster. It also lets us know that any soil that holds excess water for long periods, such as clay, is also not going to grow a very good bulb. Because bulbs are not actively growing during their dormant season, excellent drainage is required while they rest. Standing water during this time encourages rotting of the bulb.

While dormant, bulbs live off of stored energy in the form of carbohydrates and sugars. This tells us that during its growing period, a bulb requires fertile soil, proper lighting, and moisture so the plant's leaves can manufacture adequate food for itself to survive dormancy.

Drainage

Drainage is important for bulbs, and it is helpful to understand the difference between water draining through the soil and water draining off the surface of the soil. Well-drained soils that are not saturated with water will absorb normal rainfall, allowing it percolate downward. Water tends to move quickly through a good topsoil or sandy soil, because the soil particles are relatively large and have a fair amount of space between them. Because clay particles are much smaller and more tightly compacted than sand or silt, water tends to run more slowly through clay soils; and once the water permeates the soil, it becomes trapped. Clay soils also experience more surface runoff. This is why they take longer to dry out in the spring and why they are hard to resoak once they do become dry. You should be aware of the difference between common garden puddles formed by heavy rains and poorly draining soils that constantly prevent good drainage.

As mentioned previously, most spring-flowering bulbs do not like wet feet and prefer to root in open areas. Clay soils tend to stay wet in the spring; thus the bulbs die because of lack of air and excess water. Summer-flowering bulbs also require good drainage. If your soil is too clayey or too sandy, it can be improved over time with organic soil amendments. You may want to consult your local Cooperative Extension, an agency within the Department of Agriculture, for suggestions.

Testing for Soil pH

The pH value of a soil refers to the measure of its acidity on a scale of 0 to 14. The lowest end is most acid, the highest is most alkaline, and the middle (7.0) is neutral.

Most bulbs perform best in a neutral to slightly acid soil. In a soil of the correct acidity, bulbs will feed and thrive. Soil tests are the only method of determining your soil's pH. Most soil tests also reveal any nutrient shortfalls in the soil and recommend what levels of nutrients should be applied. If there is a deficiency to be corrected, it is easiest to do so during the digging process rather than after the bulbs have been planted. Again, consult your local Cooperative Extension office for details on how to get your soil tested.

Double-Digging

For the average gardener who does not have clay soils, a generous double-digging of the soil will create a perfect bulb bed. The wonderful fact is it will also create a perfect bed for any plant that is to be grown above the bulb. This is one of those rare moments when two gardening chores can be accomplished at the same time. In my garden, I find double-digging to be the perfect start for most bulbs, especially in new garden beds or beds that contain mostly annual plants. Refer to the diagram on page 13 for instructions on double-digging.

Planting in Existing Beds

I mostly grow perennials in my existing gardens, and I do not have the desire to fully double-dig the bed each time I want to add a few spring bulbs. This would mean removing all of the established plants, double-digging the bed, then replanting. For existing flower beds planted with shrubs or perennials, excavate only the area to be planted. Dig a bushel basket–sized hole, then refill it using a mix of one shovelful of compost to every three shovelsful of original soil. The trick is to dig down with the shovel a few inches deeper than you intend to plant the bottom of the bulbs. If the bottoms of the bulbs will be 8 inches deep, it is an excellent practice to dig the hole 10 to 12 inches deep and partially backfill the deep hole, using the one to three (1:3) mix, to the depth of the bottom of the bulb. Set the bulbs in and refill the rest of the hole using the same soil mix.

1. Dig a trench approximately 18 inches deep across the width of the flower bed. Remove the soil from this trench to the end of the bed or place in a wheelbarrow.

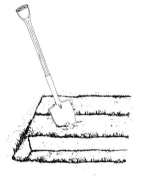

2. Then loosen the soil in the bottom of the first trench while mixing in amendments such as compost and manure.

3. Dig a second trench beside the first putting the soil from the second into the first, breaking up heavy soil clods with your shovel or spade. As the second trench is being dug and moved, for every three shovels of soil moved into the first trench, also add one of the peat moss and one of the compost.

4. Continue this trenching, filling and amending all the way down the bed. Use the soil you put aside from the first trench to fill the last one. Rake smooth, plant, and enjoy.

There is, of course, the alternate, lazy method, which is to simply plant the bulb, backfill it with the original soil, and toss some compost around the surface. I have done this with soil that is in excellent condition or that was double-dug that spring and does not require additional amendments. This has also worked well for me if the soil is fertile and has good drainage. If, however, the soil is less than satisfactory, the bulb's performance from year two onward will mirror the soil's poor condition. Note that I said from "year two onward." The first year's performance of a bulb is rarely a reflection of the growing conditions in the garden. Rather, it depends on the conditions at the originating nursery. It is the subsequent years' performances that are a result of the garden conditions. Planting a bulb is an investment in the garden for years to come, and the soil condition provides the basis for that investment.

How to Fertilize Bulbs

The "how" of fertilizing bulbs is quite simple. Most spring-flowering bulbs respond to a fertile soil but do not like to be overfed. There are two methods of feeding spring-flowering bulbs that will almost guarantee excellent performance. The first is to apply compost at a rate of 2 pounds per square foot. This is approximately half the recommended rate for application to vegetable beds. The second is to make a compost "tea" by putting several shovels of compost in an old sack and soaking the sack in a bucket of water until the water turns brown. (Omit the sack if necessary, but do let the tea steep until the water is quite brown.) This tea can be poured directly over the bulbs and will soak down to their roots. Reuse the same sack of compost until it stops turning the water brown. Naturally, any plant growing over top of the bulbs or nearby is also going to benefit from this feeding. Fish emulsion, readily available at garden centers, is an easy and effective alternate organic fertilizer if you don't want to be bothered brewing your own manure tea. This fishy concoction is my favorite all-purpose plant food.

In all the old bulb-growing manuals I have read, there is a general agreement against using any kind of fresh manure on a bulb bed. Although most of us do not have a ready source of fresh manure, it is wise to understand that fresh manure burns tender plant roots. Composted manure, purchased from garden centers is perfectly acceptable when applied at the suggested compost rate given above.

What most of us do have access to are granular fertilizers. Applying 1 or 2 pounds of nitrogen per thousand square feet will adequately feed most flowering bulbs. It is important to understand that this amount is not the amount of fertilizer to be used. It is a calculated amount based on the contents of the product being used. For example, if a product label states that the fertilizer analysis of the bag is 10–10–10, this means that 10 percent of the product is nitrogen (the first number), 10 percent is phosphorus (the second number), and 10 percent is potash (the third number). To apply 1 pound of nitrogen using a 10–10–10 fertilizer, the gardener would have to apply 10 pounds of that fertilizer. A fertilizer ratio of 10–15–15 would still require 10 pounds of fertilizer to meet the single pound of nitrogen; remember, use only the first number for calculation purposes. A fertilizer mix of 7–7–7 would require 14.3 pounds of fertilizer to add 1 pound of nitrogen (7 percent × 14.3 = 1). Here's the formula for calculating how much fertilizer to apply to bulbs, or any garden or lawn:

$$\text{Amount of bagged fertilizer to apply} = \frac{\text{Amount of nitrogen crop requires}}{\text{Percent of nitrogen in fertilizer}} \times 100$$

You can use just about any analysis of fertilizer for your bulbs if you use this formula. In practice, however, high-nitrogen, lawn-feeding fertilizers should be avoided, because it's easy to make a mistake in the application rate that would cause your plants' and bulbs' roots to be burned. Retailers sometimes sell a bulb fertilizer that has a different analysis from the regular flower fertilizer. Usually, the difference is that the bulb mix has less potash than fertilizer intended for the general flower bed. My experience is that the bulbs do not know the difference and that one kind of fertilizer does equally well on all garden plants if applied at the recommended rate. Specialty formulations are marketing devices not gardening necessities.

When to Fertilize

The next question gardeners ask is, "When do I apply compost or bulb food?" I feed bulbs at two times. The first is in the late fall after the perennial garden plant leaves have faded and most spring-flowering perennial bulbs are

COMMON SYMPTOMS OF NUTRIENT DEFICIENCIES

Element	Effect if Absent
Boron (B)	Plants are stunted; bases of young leaves become light green; stems and leaves distorted
Calcium (Ca)	Young leaves distorted; leaves irregularly shaped with edge scorching; terminal buds die
Copper (Cu)	Tips of young leaves pale and wither; leaves may fail to unfold properly or wilt easily
Iron (Fe)	Young leaves turn very pale, but all veins remain very green; brown spots may develop and leaves may become dry
Magnesium (Mg)	Older leaves first and then younger leaves turn yellowish, then reddish; tips and margins of leaves may cup upward; leaves may drop
Manganese (Mn)	Leaves turn pale, but smallest veins stay green; dead spots may appear on leaves or, in extreme cases, entire leaf may die
Nitrogen (N)	Plants grow poorly, light green in color; lower leaves may turn yellow; stems thin
Phosphorus (P)	Plants grow poorly; leaves may be bluish green with purple tints; shoot length short and thin
Potassium (K)	Older leaves may be yellow with browning at tips and scorching at margins; thin shoots.
Sulfur (S)	Young leaves pale yellow; resembles nitrogen deficiency
Zinc (Zn)	Young leaves chlorotic and then die, may show purple tones; leaves few and small, die from bottom up

making new roots. Compost is applied then so that the nutrients will work their way down to the bulb by the following spring. Granular fertilizers can also be applied in fall as well, if the gardener does not have compost. If this chore is forgotten in the rush of fall activities, it can be done as the very first spring gardening chore, before the bulbs start to push their way up. Once the bulbs are up and have finished flowering, applying compost or granular fertilizers is a waste of time because the nutrients will not leach through the soil quick enough for the bulb to make good use of them. Bulbs can be fed in the late spring if *liquid* feed is applied immediately after or during flowering. The liquid will penetrate through the soil to the bulbs and will be of use in the current growing year. Liquid fertilizer will also be absorbed through the leaves. This liquid feed can be either a compost tea or a commercial blend.

Feed summer-flowering bulbs at the same rates as spring-blooming bulbs. The difference is that an early spring feeding will be used by the summer-flowering bulbs in the year it is applied. In other words, if your want your glads and irises to look good, you have to feed them.

When to Plant

Generally, planting spring-flowering bulbs is best done six to eight weeks before the ground freezes. Exact planting times vary, depending on your gardening zone. This gives the bulbs a chance to get some roots established before the ground is too cold for root growth.

PLANTING TIMES BY ZONE

Zone Rating	Average Annual Minimum Temperature	Average Fall Planting Time
Zone 1	Below −50°F	Early September
Zone 2	Below −40°F	Early September
Zone 3	−40–30°F	September
Zone 4	−30–20°F	Late September to early October
Zone 5	−20–10°F	Late September to early October
Zone 6	−10–0°F	Mid-October
Zone 7	0–10°F	Early November
Zone 8	10–20°F	Early November
Zone 9	20–30°F	Early December; chilling needed*
Zone 10	30–40°F	Mid-December; chilling needed*
Zone 11	40°F	Late December; chilling needed*

* For a detailed description of chilling techniques, see "Temperature" on page 136.

Another question I often get is, "I've just found a package of bulbs on the shelf; can I plant them now?" The answer to this question is, "It depends." If the ground is not yet frozen, by all means get the bulbs in the ground no matter how late the planting. In this case, it is a state of nothing ventured, nothing gained. Generally, if bulbs are planted into ground that is not frozen solid, they will survive and bloom. They may not be happy about it; but because they are bulbous, with storage systems adapted for climate abuse, they will most likely survive. An interesting trick to aid survival—even if you have to use a pickax to get through the frozen surface soil to reach the unfrozen soil at bulb-planting depth—is to water the bulb heavily after planting. This watering helps the bulb establish itself in very cold ground.

If the soil is firmly frozen stiff, and the bulbs simply cannot be planted outside, then there are two things to be done. The first is to learn whether the bulbs are alive by seeing if they are still plump, not withered or dried out. If they are still hard and plump, they are likely still alive. Any softness in the bulb is a sign of death or impending death. Second, put these forgotten treasures into the crisper of the refrigerator to give them a six- to eight-week cold period; then plant them directly into a flowerpot, using a gritty potting mix; and place the pot on a sunny windowsill. The blooms will cheer up the winter household, and the bulbs will survive. Once flowering is finished, allow the green leaves to remain on the plant, and grow the bulb as a houseplant. After all danger of outside frost, plant the bulb, complete with leaves, in the garden. From then on, treat it as you would any other garden bulb.

If you're unsure whether the bulb is alive or dead, then plant it. It doesn't matter whether this is done outside during the proper time or inside after the ground has frozen solid. Look at it this way, if unplanted and thrown out, the bulb will never bloom. If planted, it may be alive and give some blooms and pleasure. Rescuing a plant from a forgotten, dusty shelf is in itself a miracle.

Ideas for Designing with Bulbs

By their very nature, gardens are personal creations, and one treads lightly when it comes to suggesting garden design changes. However, and this is a big *however*, there are some rules of thumb that will help the beginning garden designer maximize the impact of flowering bulbs.

To begin with, plant your bulbs in large groups. Or at least, in groups instead of individually. More is better. If you think about the displays of spring flowers that take your breath away, or the summer-blooming lilies that capture your eye and heart, they are always planted in masses and rarely in straight rows. Even bulbs planted in formal or geometric patterns should be spaced to avoid straight-line planting. A planting trick that helps avoid the straight-line pattern and visually increases the floral display is to place clumps of twenty or more bulbs in a triangle pattern with the tip of the triangle pointing at the garden viewer. If the triangle is slightly (very slightly) longer than wide, it will give the appearance of there being more flowers in the bed than there really are. If the garden will not hold a triangle of at least twenty bulbs, or if this quantity is unaffordable, then still try to make a clump— in any shape—of a lesser quantity to maximize the visual impact and the fragrance.

How to Cut Flowers from Your Garden

The very best time to cut flowers from bulbs is whenever you happen to be in the mood to use flowers in arrangements for the house or garden. The second best time to cut flowers is in the morning before the flower becomes dehydrated from the hot afternoon sun and wind. Cutting blossoms when they are fresh looking, newly opened, and plump with moisture helps prolong their life after being cut.

In addition, these few simple rules will help flowers last longer in the vase. To begin with, use a sharp knife instead of pruning shears to make any cuts. Sharp knives actually cut the cells of the stems, pruning shears crush them. Cut cells will continue to absorb water, and this clean water is the elixir that keeps the blooms alive. Second, cut the flower stem as low down on the stem as possible, without chopping into the base of the plant leaves. This leaves less organic matter to rot down, and it looks a lot nicer in the garden than to see a bunch of headless stems poking up like grave markers or the remains of a squirrel banquet. Once the bouquet is cut, immediately place the stems in water and recut the bottom $^1/_4$ to $^1/_2$ inch from the end. Professionals often make this second cut under water so the stem end does not dry out even for a microsecond. Moving these wet-ended stems immediately to a prepared vase full of fresh, clean water ensures that they will provide a great deal of color and enjoyment to the house.

The major exception to the rule of taking cut flowers as low down on the stem as possible is the lily. The leaves of the lily come from one central stem, and removing too many of these, especially on newly planted bulbs, will reduce needed energy production. As a rough rule of thumb, leave at least 75 percent of the stem of any newly planted lily and 50 to 60 percent on established plants.

How to Make Cut Flowers Last Longer

Will adding aspirin, soft drinks, bleach, sugar, vitamin C, or pennies to the water make your bulb flowers last longer? "Not likely," say the experts at just about every major horticultural research station. Cut flowers, except for tulips, need four things to extend their vase life: good clean water, sugars, citric acids, and antibacterial substances. They need the water to prevent dehydration and wilting. If the flower arranger snips the bottoms off the stems every second day, and does so under running water so the ends do not dry out even for an instant, water is ensured of a good pathway to the flower. Sugars feed the flower and keep it growing—except for tulips, for which it acts as an excess energy source, actually shortening the bloom's life. Researchers at the International Flower Bulb Center in Holland say that the best thing for a tulip is not to feed it but to keep the vase clean, change the water daily, and recut the stems every day or two. Fresh water, and lots of it, is the secret to long-living cut tulips.

Citric acids act as a water modifier, making the water "wetter" and allowing the stem to continue to draw up water into the flower. Use an antibacterial substance to increase the life of cut flowers by preventing bacteria from rotting the stem.

Although the use of home remedies might improve today's freshly cut flower, some research says that the improvement is temporary. Adding extra sugars or acids forces the flower to develop faster than it wants to and shortens the longevity of the bloom. Of the home remedies thought to extend flower life, none acts in all of the needed areas. At best, a lemony soft drink (like 7UP or Sprite) has both sugar and citric acid and so performs two of the main functions. Pennies might add acid and aspirins certainly do, but neither feeds the flower or prevents bacterial infection. Bleach is a good antibacterial agent, but it does not feed the flower and with carelessness can discolor household furnishings. Sugar might initially feed the plant; but without the citric acid and an antibacterial agent, the stem will quickly close up.

The best thing to be done for most cut flowers is to use a commercial cut flower powder. This provides all the necessary protection, acidity balancing, and the feeding that cut flowers require. Although they might not be as mysterious as the home remedies, these commercial blends really do work much better than anything dropped into the water from our kitchens or pockets.

A cultural tip to lengthen the vase life of cut flowers is to remove all leaves from the stems. Removing these leaves eliminates a large source of bacteria and decaying organic matter that pollutes the flower vase. Because fresh water is the single most important ingredient in long cut flower life, removing any remaining leaves is an important step.

Summer and Winter Care of Spring-Flowering Bulbs

Gardening authors like the chance to write about topics for which the rules are clear and simple. Summer care of spring bulbs is as simple as cutting off the fading or dead flowers as low down on the stalk as possible and allowing the remaining green leaves to grow until they fade or begin yellowing.

Allowing the flowers to set seed is fine in the naturalized garden in which extra plants are encouraged to establish themselves; but in the more formal garden, the plant's energies are better spent producing a healthy bulb. Although seed formation does not seriously harm the newly planted bulb, the bulb will grow larger (and hence produce better flowers) if the dead flowers are cut off. Remove spent flowers when they no longer look good by cutting their stems as if you were taking them for cut flowers (see "How to Cut Flowers from Your Garden" on page 19).

Once the leaves are well yellowed, take the pruning shears and cut them off as low to the ground as possible. Do not pull them off, even though the temptation exists, because you do not want to disturb the bulb or its shallow roots. Do not succumb to the temptation to cut the leaves off before they yellow, or the size and health of the bulb will diminish, leading to fewer or smaller flowers next year. Once the bulb leaves have been cut off, my favorite gardening maintenance rule comes into play: Forget them until the following year when they spring forth into life and bloom. Winter bulb care involves dreaming beside a roaring fireplace of the upcoming spring delights.

Summer-flowering bulbs have their own maintenance routines, which are covered in Part Four.

basic problem solving

The Essentials

- Protecting Plants from Two- and Four-Legged Pests
- Creating a Healthy Bulb Garden

Few gardening calamities equal the unexpected loss of flower buds or blossoms. After enduring winter, fresh new flower buds and leaves instill us with feelings of promised hope and beauty. When our splendid visions never become reality because of pests in the garden, the loss can sometimes be momentarily overwhelming. What follows are some accepted solutions for protecting those important spring flowers from all manner of animal, disease, and insect pests.

Protecting Plants from Two- and Four-Legged Pests

Squirrels and Chipmunks

Squirrels and chipmunks produce a huge number of complaints from gardeners. And there is almost as much lore about how to get rid of them as there are gardeners who have lost bulbs. Here are a few of the most popular and effective ways to prevent bulb and flower damage.

Feed the Critters

Some gardeners, including the White House staff, feed the squirrels and chipmunks in the fall. The idea is that if the animals are well fed with peanuts and seeds, they will have less time or inclination to bother the bulbs. This works for more than one person; Jennifer Mossop, a Toronto-area gardener, has a special feeding corner set aside in her yard for the squirrels so they will not bother her bulbs or bird feeders. She has even gone so far as to plant a stunted evergreen in that protected garden location for the rabbits to eat. "It wasn't doing well anywhere else in my garden, and it looked terrible. So now they just chew away on it; and while it never grows, it never really dies either. Now the rabbits, squirrels, and I are all happy," she explained to me as I watched her wild menagerie cavort in her backyard. Although feeding your enemy is not the solution of choice for many gardeners, it does seem to work, especially in urban areas.

The difference between the urban and rural gardens in this situation is that the urban squirrels, while sharing the same type of territory as their rural cousins, experience more population pressure and fewer predators. So, if you trap one squirrel or chipmunk, another quickly moves into the territory. In the country, squirrels have a larger territory, less competition, and more predators; thus the process of new critters restocking the garden will happen more slowly.

Clean Up the Planting Area of Bulb Debris

Although some gardeners think these engines of destruction sit in the trees and watch their lunch being planted, research suggests otherwise. Squirrels and other rodents tend to accidentally find food sources, and they really are not as organized as their reputations lead us to believe. If the debris from planting is cleaned up, they will have no reason to excavate in your bulb area.

Once the bulbs are safely planted, thoroughly water the area. This soaking creates a muddy area that the pests hesitate to work in. Plus the ground will settle sooner if it's watered, and settled ground is less likely to be bothered than freshly dug soil.

Another reason squirrels tend to excavate your bulb area is because you were digging there and left some soft dirt. These forest dwellers are not entirely without reason; digging to them means food burying. If they can find another animal's cache, then they are one up on that other creature in the natural fight for survival. Unfortunately, we are the other animal, and we have buried our treasures in the squirrels' area. We have also planted enough bulbs and left the ground turned over in a large enough area that even a low-wattage squirrel is smart enough to notice. A way to thwart this instant digging is to cover the area with an old window screen, weighted down so that the rodent cannot move it. After thoroughly watering in the bulbs (which, remember, is an excellent thwarting mechanism by itself), lay screens over the area until the ground is well settled.

Deep Planting and Added "Seasonings"

Deep planting is a technique that works for tulips. If the bulbs are planted deeper than the rodents are willing to dig, they will remain safe. The bulbs must be placed at a depth that does not affect their growth and flowering; planting 10 to 12 inches deep is recommended.

Some gardeners swear by mixing specific products into the ground around the planting holes or by spreading the products singly or in combination around the surface after planting. I have heard of garlic, cayenne pepper, black pepper, ammonia, hot pepper seeds, and mothballs all being strewn about the garden to halt the depredation. Each of these methods has its proponents and its naysayers. None has ever worked for me. In fact, a gardener who asks to remain nameless says she has seen squirrels carrying her carefully distributed mothballs around in their mouths. Her next comments are unprintable.

Gadgets: Sprinklers and Electronics

Several other methods have their supporters. The first is a water sprinkler system controlled by a motion detector. Once the motion detector senses movement, it activates a solenoid valve that in turn sends water to a sprinkler head; the intruder is doused with a fifteen-second burst of water. This may work better on cats and mail carriers than it does on squirrels, but there are folks who sing its praises and claim their bulbs were never better. This does have the advantage of protecting not only the planted bulbs but also the emerged flowers the following spring. Motion-controlled sprinklers are available at garden centers and are sometimes called electronic scarecrows.

Electronics are finding their way into the garden in other ways as well, and some manufacturers claim to have ultrasonic devices that repel squirrels, chipmunks, cats, and dogs. The best of these are hooked up to motion detectors so that the animals do not become accustomed to the sound. These electronic gizmos have their proponents. Although I have never used one in my own garden, I have many radio listeners who claim they work well. The systems are available from pest-protection businesses.

Screens

Screen planting is one of those gardening tricks picked up from somewhere that deserves special recognition. It is used when nothing else will stop rodents from digging up and destroying bulbs. Merely dig a hole broader than deep in which to plant your bulbs. Set the bulbs in the bottom of the hole, and then cover them with $^1/_2$ inch of soil. After the shallow layer of soil, cover the bulbs with $^1/_2$-inch hardware cloth, and finish backfilling with soil. The wire hardware cloth, available at any good hardware or building supply store, is tough enough to prevent rodents from cutting through it to reach the bulbs, yet the holes are wide enough to allow the bulb flower stalk to work its way through to reach the surface and produce spring flowers. Do plant the bulbs a few inches deeper than normal if wire screening is used. Subsequent digging and planting in the area will be easier if the screening is not being hit every time a trowel or cultivator is put in the ground.

The downside of this is that the bulbs are virtual prisoners, and removing them and the wire mesh is almost as time-consuming as planting them. If nothing else has worked, however, this method will. Some gardeners I know have even gone as far as bending the edges of the hardware cloth down to form a box over the bulbs. They now have to protect only the flowers, not the bulbs.

Sprays

Chemical sprays applied to the bulbs before planting work well. Squirrels and chipmunks do not like the taste of the chemical and avoid eating the bulb. Using a spray on every bulb is a time-consuming and somewhat messy job, but many of these sprays (with wonderful names, such as Not in My Backyard) work well. They were originally developed to protect electrical wires and systems from being eaten by squirrels and have been adapted to bulbs and flowers by clever marketing.

The Family Pet

Cats and dogs work as well. Using a larger predator to control a smaller one is a time-honored gardening trick. Even if the cat or dog cannot catch the squirrel, the presence of the larger animal is often enough to turn the trick by constant chasing. In my gardens, I used to have almost complete control of mice and chipmunks through my resident barn cat population. Then I got a new dog that chases the cats!

Moles and Voles

Moles and voles are another source of frustration for bulb growers and their surrounding lawns. The practical difference between moles and voles is quite simple. Moles are carnivorous and eat lawn grubs but rarely flowers. They do damage by disturbing the plants as they tunnel around looking for grubs and worms. Voles, on the other hand, are vegetarian and do not eat grubs. The seem to prefer the plants in your garden to any other botanic delight. There are some very sound and easily followed gardening practices that will reduce or eliminate the damage from these pests.

Control can focus on either eliminating voles and moles or discouraging them from eating the bulb. Elimination of the rodent itself is often the direction chosen by most gardeners, as these pests do not have the same cuteness factor possessed by their squirrel and chipmunk cousins. The horticulture literature is full of advertisements for devices to trap, impale, and behead these subterranean eating machines. I have never had much luck with these devices, but I do know gardeners who crow over each successful capture. I prefer to work in a less direct method.

I have found several things that work well to send moles on their merry way. The first is to eliminate their main source of food. Because they do eat a lot of lawn grubs, getting rid of the grubs encourages them to leave the area in search of a better food source. Although there are chemical compounds sold in garden shops for this purpose, a very effective organic solution is to use predator nematodes.

Nematodes are naturally occurring, microscopic, wormlike creatures that eat almost every stationary larva in the soil. They eat almost two hundred different types of lawn and garden pests, at no danger to beneficial earthworms (veritable speed demons in the underworld), nematodes offer an environmentally friendly solution to many garden problems. Applied at the recommended rate, which is millions of microscopic nematodes to a thousand square feet of lawn or garden, they are efficient predators who leave few living larvae in their wake. Because they themselves are so tiny, they do not travel farther than 1 or 2 feet in a season. Once they eat all the grubs and larvae in their area, they starve to death. This returns their numbers to naturally occurring population levels. Their control life lasts only a single season, and they in turn are in no danger of permanently upsetting the natural ecology. With the elimination of the grubs, not only do the rodents tend to move away but the lawn and garden plants will be healthier because nothing is eating their roots. Nematodes are available in the spring and summer from reputable garden centers.

Another organic technique for getting rid of lawn grubs (and hence moles) is to soak the lawn or bulb area with castor oil. I originally read this in a garden magazine from the 1800s, but now there are commercial preparations of castor oil available for sale through garden centers. Mixed at approximately 10 parts of water to 1 part of castor oil and poured through a watering can onto the area to be protected, this old remedy still works to chase away grubs and their predators. There is even some anecdotal evidence that the remaining smell deters aboveground pests such as raccoons and skunks.

If the bulbs are being eaten in the ground by voles, the best of these modern gardening tips is to soak the bulb in a terrible-tasting concoction before planting. There are commercially available products developed specifically for treating bulbs before they are planted. Once soaked or sprayed and allowed to dry, the bulb can be treated and planted normally. Do not wipe your face with your hands while working with these products. You won't like the taste either.

A product for deterring both underground rodents that has just come onto the market is an ultrasonic torpedo. The pointed end of this cylindrical device is stuck in the ground, the batteries are turned on, and the torpedo ultrasonically hums away. According to Frank Karnick, who had a place in New Milford, Connecticut, this device saved his garden. He described how they lost every flower they planted one year to moles and voles. The garden annuals were decimated, and none survived. The next year they installed one of these torpedoes, and they've never lost a plant since. Trying to be fair as an evaluator, he went on to suggest that perhaps all the moles moved away or died over the winter or got caught by a cat; but the only difference thing that he and his wife did differently was to use the ultrasonic torpedo. He said if you put your ear down to it, you can hear it humming away; and the only thing he knows is that there are no mole problems while it is running. The ultrasonic torpedo is available through garden magazines, mail-order catalogs, and garden centers.

Protecting Flowers from Rodents

An almost larger problem than protecting the bulbs is protecting the flowers once they have started to appear in the spring. I have heard more laments about damaged flowers or disappearing buds than I ever thought possible. Even the sanest of gardeners go berserk when the long-awaited flowers are cut through and toppled like sheaves of wheat on a prairie landscape. Or stalks stand beheaded, like bare fence posts, where colorful flowers once graced the garden.

Some of the following suggestions definitely work, and others seem to work for only some people. The only thing I have ever found to really work to stop a four-legged creature—whether chipmunk, squirrel, or groundhog— from eating flower buds or the opened flowers themselves is a vile-tasting spray regularly applied to the bud as it emerges and develops. One nearby friend had a "pet" groundhog living off the edge of her property and could not bring herself to eliminate it. Once she was introduced to the spraying program idea, she had flowers survive for the first time in years.

The secret to any of the available sprays, whether homemade or commercially purchased, is to apply them as soon as the shoots begin to appear and regularly afterward at almost every new stage of growth. The plan in this is to make sure that when the grazing animal takes the very first bite, it will not like the taste. If the animal doesn't like the first taste, it tends to avoid the plant for the rest of the season. If the pest likes the first unsprayed bite, it tends to keep chewing off everything, even the terrible-tasting ones, because it just *knows* there is a good-tasting one in there somewhere. This is why gardeners will often see a row of flowers cut off and lying on the ground—the small creature is out there looking for a good tasting morsel and has not found it yet . . . but it keeps on looking! It seems that these small engines of destruction can hold only one thought in their heads at a time; and if that thought is of foul-tasting flowers instead of pleasant-tasting flowers, then the gardener wins the battle. Naturally, this is a gardening practice that must be rigorously followed every year to be effective.

The following personal experience is added here as a note to those fighting off groundhogs. I can testify that human male urine, placed down the hole of groundhogs, is an effective deterrent. Groundhogs tend to move away from the areas, abandoning the holes, in which this happens regularly. I have moved the entire groundhog population of my farm out of and away from my vegetable garden. I do not care if they tuck into the grasses and clovers in the fields, I just do not want them eating my flowers and vegetables. I will leave it to your imagination about how to get the urine down the hole.

Birds

Many of us enjoy birds in our gardens and we go to a lot of trouble to encourage them to visit us all winter. We just wish they would go somewhere else to pick away at emerging spring flowers. Nothing comes without a price in the garden. Most bird-watching gardeners cheerfully pay the price; but if the limit of your cheerfulness has been reached, you might try a few of these solutions. I have to confess right off the top that I willingly pay the price for birds in my garden; and except for the eyeball, described below, I have not used any technique to get rid of birds. The following methods have been described by my customers and friends.

Get a white, medium-sized ball, perhaps the size of a bowling ball, and paint a large, single eye in the middle of the ball that takes up the entire side. I'm told by those that have experimented with this that anything semi-round, such as an old white pie plate, will work as well. The important thing is to make sure the painted eye is large and contrasts well with the color of the background. Attach the ball to a stake or string and put it in the garden. Research has shown the single eye to be more effective at scaring away birds than any of the commercially available plastic owls or other stuffed predators.

Gardeners tell me that moving plastic snakes around the garden also works for them; but my daughter hates snakes, plastic or otherwise, so I do not put plastic ones in our garden. That way she knows any snake she sees is real, and she should jump.

Although it may sound cruel, a larger predator such as a dog or cat will keep birds away from garden flower beds. Electronic devices that make ultrasonic or distressed bird calls have been known to work for some gardeners.

Dogs and Cats

Garden authors are often asked to provide solutions to wandering dogs and cats. In my experience, any solution that stops dogs enrages half the animal-loving population; and the solution that stops cats, makes the other half mad. You cannot win for trying. I'm told that gardeners rush in where angels fear to tread; therefore . . .

Dogs are more easily barred from the garden than are cats. If it is your own dog, then training is a possibility as is one of the various electronic containment systems. These work wonderfully well to discourage the household animals from visiting protected areas. I have found that it takes only a few days of training before the dogs get the picture and will not trespass into protected areas. Anstace and Larry Esmonde-White of PBS's gardening show *From a Country Garden* installed one when the system first arrived on the market to control their two enthusiastic retrievers. As Anstace said, "It worked so well that the dogs have never worn the collars again; all that money and it only took a few days." Visible fences work for dogs as well. Dogs can be trained not to jump over short fences; although from personal experience, I know it takes more training for some dogs than for others.

Controlling wandering strays is another problem. Fences can be of either conventional solid and tall construction or of electric wire. Small electric fences, similar to farm cattle fences, are often sold at garden centers as a way of protecting a garden area from all wandering dogs. Generally, a dog will be stung only once by one of these fences before it avoids the area. If the fences are to be barriers, they do have to be tall enough that dogs can't jump over them and complete enough (no openings) so the dogs can't find an entrance. Naturally, any dog fence can be disguised with vines or other flowering plants to reduce its ugliness.

Some dogs do not like the electronic scarecrow controller that shoots water at them. On the other hand, if the dog is like my young Labrador retriever, this is not a control, it is a toy.

Controlling cats is another matter. These creatures can climb most fences, so fencing is really not an option. On the other hand, the scarecrow water sprinkler route is almost assured, because it is a very rare cat that enjoys an unexpected shower. Some gardeners use a cocoa bean mulch to prevent cats digging in their garden. Apparently cats do not like the rolling texture and avoid this material.

Another method is to observe the cat entering and leaving the garden; most cats tend to enter the area from the same place each time. Sink a metal can filled with ammonia into the cat's path to act as a deterrent. This has to be replenished regularly if it is to be effective, because cats do not like the heavy ammonia smell. Keeping the garden soil well watered is also a deterrent reported by many gardeners; cats do not like mud. Then again, many plants do not like the excess water either.

You can also purchase an electronic deterrence system that produces a high-frequency sound that works on cats and dogs alike. The best of these are controlled by a motion detector, so the animals are startled by the sound each time it comes on. I have no personal experience with these systems; but some of my radio listeners swear by them. The best of these electronic devices have switches that allow you to change the frequency, depending on the pest to be chased away.

Even Bigger Pests—Deer

Deer destroyed my apple orchard, and this is not at all unusual in our neighborhood. What was unusual was the orchard was only a few yards from our back door. This apparently presented no problem to these nocturnal visitors who, I can honestly report, liked all fourteen apple varieties equally well. Deer control for bulb flowers is limited to only a few weeks of the year; even a deer is not going to bother a bulb in January.

There are a few products around that provide some measure of control. The first of these is human urine. This might seem unusual, but it works. If human urine is spread at the entrance point to the garden, it effectively marks the territory; and the deer will avoid the garden if possible. This marking has to be repeated regularly if it is to be effective. Marking is most easily done by the male in the family, especially between quarters or periods of televised sports during the spring bulb-blooming period.

Repeatedly, articles in magazines report that hanging balls of hair or bars of soap in trees will repel deer. Many of my friends say that these are temporary solutions at best, and after a few spring rains there is little if any deterrent value. The jury on things like zoo-poo says much the same. Regularly replenished, they may work well. All of these deterrents, from urine to soap, work well if the deer have easily available alternate sources of food. With few food alternatives, deer are not easily deterred by a few unusual smells.

Fencing is a solution that works. There are new deer fences on the market that are tall, strong, and nearly invisible to the human eye. Deer hesitate to jump when they cannot see the fence. The fences themselves are easily installed; see "Bulb Sources" on page 144 for mail-order sources.

Creating a Healthy Bulb Garden

It is my personal experience that a relaxed attitude toward gardening is one of the most beneficial tools that a new gardener can cultivate. Bringing type A behavior to the garden defeats the purpose of gardening. Gardening is supposed to be relaxing, not a problem that requires another compulsive burst of activity. There will be losses—both of bulbs and of flowers—that are inevitable. If you accept that these losses are only a small part of the natural cycle in the garden and that there are many other life forms out there as well, all struggling to survive, then the place of one or two flowers or bulbs becomes easier to put into perspective. To really enjoy the garden, imagine that each flower exists within an environmental circle, a fully functioning microenvironment. This environment comes complete with beneficial predators to eat the bad bugs; but for the beneficials to survive, there must be a supply of bad bugs. And, unfortunately, the food source that keeps the bad bugs alive is your plants. There is a price to be paid in the garden, and sometimes it is your flowers.

After twenty years of experimenting, reading, and gardening, I have arrived at a relaxed but committed approach to the health of my garden. The garden's health is directly tied to my own; the healthier I can make my soil and garden, the healthier the environment that surrounds me. And that's a good feeling. The plants grow better, and the food I eat from the garden is wholesome and delicious. Although this is beginning to sound very much like a sermon, it does all come back to several practical gardening tips.

Feed the Soil and Not the Plants

Remember to feed the soil, not the plants. To do this, add copious amounts of compost. Compost is indeed the lifeblood of any gardening soil. After several years of adding as much compost as recommended (see "How to Fertilize Bulbs" on page 14), the plants will be healthier and the incidence of diseases and invading pests will begin to slow down. Healthy plants do not attract problems as frequently as do struggling plants. Chemical fertilizers do not have the same positive impact as compost on soil life and health; if in doubt—use compost.

Mulch Your Plants with an Organic Mulch

Use an organic mulch and celebrate as it is absorbed into the soil of the garden, even if it costs money to replace the mulch as it decays. This organic breakdown is feeding the microorganisms that are working to create a healthy soil. The insects seen wandering around under the mulch may indeed be eating the mulch (earwigs especially love to munch away on decomposing organic matter), but they too are part of the plan. Organic matter can be broken down for plant use through more than one route, and one of those roots is through insects' digestive systems. I notice that in my garden the earwigs pretty much stay below the mulch layers instead of climbing up my flowers looking for decaying organic matter to eat. Although some gardeners complain of earwigs eating their flowers, this insect's preferred food is decaying organic matter. Provide this in the form of mulch, and the flowers will generally be left alone. This is only one example of creating an environment that promotes health in the garden. Using compost and mulch together creates an environment in which many more beneficial relationships will occur.

Use Organic Pest and Disease Control Methods

The literature is full of stories and experiments, both pro and con, for the use of synthetic and organic control methods. Groups on each side of the issue rail against those on the other side, despite scientific results and philosophical differences. My reason for using organic methods is quite simple. They work. I also know they do not hurt my specific environment. After all, this is my personal garden: I live here, I roll on the ground here, my kids and dogs play here and track garden dust and dirt into the house. With the organic controls I use, there is no problem with either my personal environment or my relationship with my neighbors and the larger community. The controls are described in "Problem Solving," below.

PROBLEM SOLVING

Problem	Likely Cause
PEST, DISEASE, AND ENVIRONMENTAL AND CULTURAL DAMAGE	
Flower stalks but no buds	Birds, chipmunks, or squirrels eating the buds.
No flower stalks but lots of healthy leaves; no bud formation	Bulb does not have enough stored energy. The foliage may have been cut off too early, the bulb may be growing in the shade, there may not be enough food present in the soil, or there was too much water during the summer.
No leaves or flower stalks from planted bulbs	Dead bulb. If recently planted, the bulb could have been eaten by rodents or birds, or you could have planted a diseased bulb or planted too late. If established planting, you may have overwatered or the garden area may have become too shady.
Leaves dwarfed and yellowish green	Botrytis mold, caused by the *Botrytis* fungus, the most common fungus problem. Bulbs may have been planted in shady, moist areas or areas without adequate ventilation, which are perfect environments for fungus development.
Leaves flecked with brown spots at bloom time; no earlier frost damage	Botrytis mold.
Flowers discolored with gray mottling; rotting petals	Botrytis mold.
Leaves turn red; leaves wilt and die early; no flowers or small, stunted blooms	Basal rot. The bulb was likely infected by the commercial grower when dug or stored.

Put Gardening in Perspective

Accept the loss of a flower, plant, or bulb with grace. It is, after all, only a flower. In the relative scheme of things, it is not worth high blood pressure or a heart attack. Compared to any single item on the evening news, a lost flower pales in significance. The garden is a magical place, enjoy it for what exists within it and do not fret for what is lost.

Solution
See pages 26 and 33 for control methods.
This is a cultural problem, not a disease; see Part One for cultural information.
See "Protecting Plants from Two- and Four-Legged Pests" on page 26, "How to Buy Bulbs" on page 2, "When to Plant" on page 17, and Part One for cultural information.
Move plants to sunny, well-draining, open beds. For annual bulbs, remove dead debris regularly during the growing season and spray with fungicide; after the growing season, dry and store properly. For perennial bulbs, rigorously remove dead or dying leaves and flower bud debris; maintain a fungicide program all growing season.
See above.
See above.
There is no cure; it is best to discard the bulb, particularly if you live in the Pacific Northwest. See "How to Buy Bulbs" on page 2. If desired, bulbs can be soaked in a fungicide; air dry bulb before planting.

continues

Problem	Likely Cause
Stored bulbs are dull and/or white; and basal plate is quite shrunken	Basal rot.
Flower stalks shrivel below or near the leaf axils	Stem rot or flower spot, caused by the *Phytophthora* fungus. Usually occurs when there is poor ventilation, lack of sunlight, and sometimes excessive moisture.
Striping of tulip blooms that aren't supposed to be bicolor	Tulip breaking virus.
Oval or oblong spots on leaves or flowers after a cold spell early in season	Frost injury. Although uncommon, it can occur after a cold spell in the early spring.
Flower stalk and stem collapses on tulips	Topple injury. A physiologic problem; some varieties are more prone than others. Usually caused by insufficient ripening of the bulb the previous summer (normally after a cool, wet year); often caused by clayey soil; sometimes the result of excessively high spring temperatures. Some taller, later varieties suffer from wind damage.
Base of purchased bulb is moldy	Blue mold rot caused by *Penicillium* spp. Often a secondary infestation after bulb mite damage.
Stem or bulb rots	A variety of agents; generally the result of poor cultural practices. Double tulips grown in shady or poorly ventilated areas are susceptible.
Narcissus leaves and flowers are spotted and rotting	Fire fungus. This fungus loves rainy springs; it does not harm the bulb but ruins the flower and foliage.

INSECTS

Small, green, or black bugs, mostly in colonies; black sooty mold on plant	Aphids (tulip bulb aphid, crescent-marked lily aphid, peach aphid).

See page 39, "Basal rot."

Dig up bulbs and replant in a better location to relieve overcrowding, increase sunlight, or improve drainage. No spray control is recommended.

No cure. Dig out and destroy all infected bulbs, because they will infect the others, eventually weakening the bulb colony.

No cure, except a warmer climate. Do not confuse with fungus attack: Frost damage occurs very early in season after cold spell, whereas fungal problems usually occur later in growing season when the weather warms.

No cure or treatment; see Part One for cultural information.

Best to avoid buying damaged bulbs; see "How to Buy Bulbs" on page 2. Bulbs can be dipped in fungicide, air dried, and planted. Treat annual bulbs to eliminate possible mite damage; see below.

Not common. Discard rotted bulbs to reduce infestation. Move survivors into a sunny and windy spot. See Part One for cultural information.

Prevention is the best cure; remove and discard all dead leaves after spring growth is finished. Spray with fungicide weekly in the spring if rain is very frequent and past infestations have occurred. The spots are distinct in that they stand out from green foliage; there are usually visible spores clustered together on the stalks.

Most aphids can be destroyed with insecticidal soap or a determined squish of the gardener's fingers.

continues

Problem	Likely Cause
Tulip has yellow leaves and flowers that don't open or are stunted	Bulb mites. These insects survive underground and are difficult to treat.
Iris or gladiolus has yellow leaves and flowers that don't open or are stunted	Thrips. These insects eat away the soft tissue of the blossom; the lesions produce fluid that feeds the thrip. Thrips overwinter on stored glad corms.
Lower buds are stunted and don't open; upper buds may be fine	Tarnished plant bug.
Chewed-out bulbs	White grubs.
Small swellings of yellowish tissue on leaves that are worse in shady areas; mostly a narcissus problem	Stem and bulb nema.
Shoots turn yellow and become deformed and stunted; mostly a gladiolus problem	Wireworms. This brown, long, narrow, hard-shelled beetle larvae will also bore holes at base of the leaves and flower stalk.

Solution

Never plant bulbs that are known to be infested with mites. There is no soil sterilizer; but repeated (every 2–3 days) applications of insecticidal soap to the developing leaves, buds, and flowers may knock them back. For annual bulbs, dip in insecticidal soap for 5 minutes to reduce mites; rinse and dry before planting.

Spray weekly with insecticidal soap from time of leaf emergence to bud formation. Use rotenone or pyrethrum dusts where past infestations have occurred. Corms and bulbs can be soaked in a mixture of $1^1/_4$ tablespoons of Lysol in 1 gallon of water for 3 hours just before planting to reduce thrips.

Eliminate this common garden bug's overwintering sites, such as weed or garden debris piles. Regular application of rotenone or pyrethrum dusts will control.

Nematodes will control lawn grubs; see "Moles and Voles" on page 30.

Identify infestation by cutting the bulb in half; infected bulbs have dark colored circles rather than a white interior. Discard badly infected bulbs. Lift other bulbs after growth stops, removing all dirt, and store them dry and cool for summer. Drying kills the microscopic nema worm. Or put the bulbs in hot water (110°F exactly) for 3 hours, stirring often; do not overcook (which kills the bulbs along with the mites and nemas). Replant immediately.

Identify by lifting bulbs; eaten sections will be very visible. Do not plant bulbs in clay soils. A soil drench with an appropriate chemical may be needed for severe infestations. Consult your local Agricultural Extension agent for a registered product.

easy spring bloomers

The Essentials

- How to Figure Out When Your Bulbs Will Bloom
- Plant Portraits for Easy Spring Bloomers

The Greek gods sport in flower-filled Elysium, Wordsworth ponders fields of daffodils, and modern gardeners dream of spring garden photography: We all share the love of spring blossoms. Flowers spell the end of winter in our gardens; and for no other reason than that, they are welcome to our winter-weary psyches. Spring-flowering bulbs exist for every garden and almost every garden location—from the cutting garden to the rock garden. Whether naturalized in open spaces, massed in perennial borders, or tucked in the small spaces near the house, they usher spring to our gardens with a painter's palette of color. Spring bulbs can do it all. The plants on these pages were chosen because they are easily found in catalogs and garden centers. The reason they are easily found is that they are, for the most part, the easiest bulbs to grow. Furthermore, they have the best flowering habits and give a great color show for the least amount of work. These are reasons enough for me to have them in my garden and to encourage you to include them in yours.

One problem that many beginning gardeners face is trying to decide when these plants will bloom in their gardens. For example, just when does an early tulip bloom? When does a midseason or Kaufmanniana tulip bloom? It is difficult to write a guide for the season of bloom of each bulb, because blooming cycles are relative to your own climate. A bulb that flowers early in Virginia will be blooming several weeks later in northern New York; but for the colder climate, it is still considered early.

How to Figure Out When Your Bulbs Will Bloom

Each of the following plant portraits includes a flowering date for a particular gardening zone. To find out roughly when the plant will bloom in your garden use this system: Determine the difference between your gardening zone and the one listed. If you live in a colder climate (lower zone number) than the one listed, add one week for each zone difference; if you live in a warmer climate (higher zone number), subtract one week for each zone difference. For example, suppose the plant portrait notes that an early tulip regularly blooms in the second week of May in zone 4. If you live in zone 6 (a warmer climate), you can expect the same type of tulip to bloom in your area in the last week of April; the two-zone difference equals about a two-week difference in bloom time. If you live in zone 2 (a colder climate), you can expect this plant to bloom at the end of May. While this is not a rigid rule, because spring conditions vary from year to year and area to area, it is a good approximation. See the USDA Hardiness Zone Map on page 150 to find your gardening zone. I hasten to acknowledge that zones are not carved in stone but are simply useful guidelines for those of us experimenting with new plants and garden ideas.

Plant Portraits for Easy Spring Bloomers

Allium

Onion
Height: 8–48 inches
Bloom Time: Very early spring through early summer
Depth to Plant: 4 inches
Spacing: 2 inches for short bulbs; 8–12 inches for tall bulbs
Best Season to Plant: Fall
Sunlight Needed: Full sun

Alliums are onions by any other name; and within the horticultural specialist's world, those who collect alliums are often kidded about growing a bunch of "nasty" flowers. The key point, for us nonspecialists, is that alliums have flowers—wonderful flowers—and delightful seedpods that give a long season of usefulness that is not matched by too many other plants. They are well worth growing, and the described species are easily found at garden centers and through mail-order catalogs.

There are two kinds of alliums, those that live mainly in the temperate Northern Hemisphere and those found in the Southern Hemisphere. There are some differences between them that should be noted by gardeners. The most important is that the onions from the Northern Hemisphere form bulbs and grow well when the summers are dry; on the other hand, those from the Southern Hemisphere grow from rhizomes and like ample moisture during the summer.

The northern temperate bulbs tend to like dry summers bracketed by good growing moisture in the spring and fall. In the wild, they are normally found in dry, rocky terrain rather than in a rich gardenlike soil. In the gardens, they are best suited for rougher design areas or rock gardens. If planted along with perennials in borders, they must be put in areas where they will not receive too much water and fertilizer during the summer, which can cause them to rot. Some species, such as *A. giganteum* and *A. christophii* (*A. albopilosum*), make wonderful border plants if properly cared for, because they come in a range of colors; although, to be fair, the colors do tend to the purple, violet, and pink spectrum.

For best results, plant the hardy allium bulbs in the full sun and allow ample spring and fall moisture. Plant them in an area with excellent drainage, so that summer rains do not soften and rot the bulb tissue. Clay soils, because they hold moisture for too long, are not recommended for alliums. Before describing some specific bulbs, it should be noted that alliums are, for the most part, easily grown from seed. They can be started just like tiny onions if the seed is purchased from specialty seed catalogs. Once in the garden, they do tend to self-sow, producing abundant seeds. If happy in their sunny spot, they may even become a bit of a nuisance. Luckily, alliums are easily picked out and shared among friends. Some species are even edible as chives (*A. schoenoprasum*), Welsh onions (*A. fistulosum*), Canada garlic (*A. canadense*), wild onion (*A. cernuum*), and culinary garlic (*A. sativum*).

Members of the second class of alliums have more of a rhizome-type root system and come from areas where summer rainfall is abundant, such as the Himalayas and East Asia. Because the northern bulb species are generally the most attractive alliums, the southern species are rarely offered in catalogs. They are, however, available through some specialist seed companies and may become more available as the South African species are introduced to cultivation. If a summer moisture–loving allium is allowed to dry out in the garden, its life span will be shortened. Tender southern alliums prefer full sun but demand summer water if they are to survive and flower well. The rhizome, however, still requires good drainage and should not be planted in clay soils, because a dry period of dormancy during the winter months is necessary to develop flower buds and leaves. This class of alliums is best grown in the warmer portions of the continent and ignored in the more northern regions.

Short alliums grow well in rock gardens and display beds where they are not shaded by overhanging foliage. The taller varieties, such as *A. giganteum,* are showstoppers in the main perennial garden. As with most bulbs, plant alliums in clumps to create a stunning effect. This is particularly true with any of the smaller or shorter alliums; they need lots of company to create an impact.

A. christophii (A. albopilosum)

Height: 24 inches
Bloom Time: First week of June in zone 4
Depth to Plant: 4–6 inches
Spacing: 4 inches
Best Season to Plant: Fall
Sunlight Needed: Full sun

Allium christophii

A. christophii is also sold as *A. albopilosum.* Sometimes plant taxonomists (the scientists that name plants) cannot quite agree on a Latin name or cannot convince plant sellers that they should change plant names. You will see this allium listed either way and sometimes both. The first time I saw this plant (a native of Persia, now Turkey and Iran), I fell in love with its amazing seedpods and their huge, airy, starlike shapes—hence its common name, star of Persia. Metallic purple florets make up the umbel on this plant, and its beauty during late spring fills the gap nicely as the tulip blooms decline. An excellent plant for the front of the perennial border, it is hardy into zone 3.

A. giganteum

Height: 48 inches

Bloom Time: Second week of June in zone 4

Depth to Plant: 4–6 inches

Spacing: 8–10 inches

Best Season to Plant: Fall

Sunlight Needed: Full sun

A. giganteum, a native of central Asia, was introduced to gardeners late in the 1800s and has been popular ever since. Its 6-inch flower umbels, held on stiff, upright stems reach 4–6 feet in height, giving it a garden presence unknown to its smaller cousins. It is quite hardy, easily grown, and affected by few pests. A small clump of four to six bulbs is a showstopper in most gardens. Plant bulbs at least 8 inches apart. A joker friend used to spray the still-standing but faded seed heads in his garden with gold paint. This amused him and confused more than one horticulturally correct visitor to his garden. Plant breeders are using *A. giganteum* to give some extra height and size to their hybrid plants. One example of this is the cultivar 'Globemaster', a cross between *A. giganteum* and *A. stipitatum* (native to Afghanistan through to Russia). 'Globemaster' has 10-inch, silver-violet blossoms and will be a hit in any garden.

A. karataviense

Height: 8 inches

Bloom Time: Second week of May in zone 4

Depth to Plant: 3–4 inches

Spacing: 3 inches

Best Season to Plant: Fall

Sunlight Needed: Full sun

This central Asian species, found in the Black Mountain range in Kazakhstan, has a bluish-green leaf topped with a 6-inch umbel. An umbel is a flower composed of smaller flowers whose stalks all start at the same place; and alliums all have umbels as a flower form. Each flower part in the umbel ranges from white to pale purplish pink; the overall effect is a dull white. The interesting thing about this allium is that the flower stalk is almost nonexistent so the umbel appears to be resting directly on the foliage. A wonderful addition to the rock garden, although it can get lost in the main perennial garden.

A. moly

Height: 10 inches
Bloom Time: Fourth week of May in zone 4
Depth to Plant: 3–4 inches
Spacing: 4 inches
Best Season to Plant: Fall
Sunlight Needed: Full sun

Allium moly

The yellow onion has a wonderful yellow umbel and self-sows happily enough that it soon covers a good territory with its bright cheerful blooms. A native to southern and southeastern Europe, it is hardy down to zone 2 or 3, depending on the specific location. Easily grown from seed or purchased bulbs, it is a welcome addition to the front of the perennial border. The cultivar 'Jeannine' is an improved version, because it has two stems per bulb rather than the single stem typical of the species.

Anemone blanda

Windflower

Height: 12 inches
Bloom Time: Fourth week of April to first week of
    May in zones 5–6
Depth to Plant: 4 inches
Spacing: 4–6 inches
Best Season to Plant: Fall (see text)
Sunlight Needed: Full sun to part shade

Anemone blanda

Anemone varieties come in three main groups. Two of these are spring-flowering tuberous-rooted forms, and the third has a fibrous root system. The spring-flowering tuberous forms are dealt with here and summer-blooming types are described in Part Four.

A. *blanda* varieties are naturally found in woodland edges, or high meadows. They like a moist but well-drained soil with lots of humus and will tolerate, but not appreciate, dry summer conditions. These are perfect general garden plants and thrive in good garden soils with adequate summer moisture. Their normal range is zones 5 through 8, and gardeners in colder or warmer areas than these will find windflowers difficult to keep alive or bloom. The cultivar 'Blue Star' has hyacinth blue blooms, 'Pink Star' has pale pink blooms with a lighter center, and 'Violet Star' has violet blooms with a white center eye. Plant *A. blanda* in the fall with the other fall-planted bulbs; it will flower quite early in the spring if it is planted in a zone where it will survive. Like most bulbs, the *Anemone* species do not like standing water or clay soils.

Chionadoxa luciliae

Glory-of-the-Snow
Height: 3–8 inches
Bloom Time: Third to fourth week of April in zone 4
Depth to Plant: 1–2 inches
Spacing: 2–3 inches
Best Season to Plant: Fall
Sunlight Needed: Full sun to very light shade

Chionadoxa luciliae

Glory-of-the-snow is one of the earliest bulbs to bloom in the garden. The genus name *Chionadoxa* comes from the Greek *chion,* meaning "snow," and *doxa,* meaning "glory." Glory-of-the-snow is an apt name because in climates warmer than zone 4, it may even appear through the snow; or at least that is what all the books say. But in my zone 4 garden, my bulbs are smart enough to wait until the snow has melted over top of them before they appear. To their credit, late snowfalls and frost do not hurt them, but in my garden they do not poke up through the ice and snow as some authors suggest. I have seen pictures of these flowers in their native habitat surrounded by snow melt. In other words, they were in a large, cleared section of rocky turf, surrounded by still-melting snow. Perhaps they are very early but not invincible. Native to Turkey and Cypress, these bulbs are excellent for the rock garden. Their small size easily gets lost among the large plants of the main border, so plant glory-of-the-snow where they can easily be seen, enjoyed, and maintained. The cultivars range in color from shades of blue through pinks and whites. All are interesting and early enough to be included in any list of bulbs for the color-starved gardener.

Crocus

Crocus

The *Crocus* genus includes many bulbs that have an extended bloom time in warmer climates, making them a very valuable addition to the garden. This bulb has a long history of cultivation; for example, *C. sativus* is an important commercial source of yellow dye; its first recorded use was in Crete in 1500 B.C. The medicinal value of the same plant was recorded in Kashmir in 500 B.C.; and it is still commercially cultivated in Spain, India, Russia, and China. Crocus species can be divided into two, based on bloom time: spring and fall. The commonly available fall-blooming species are described on page 128.

Crocus can be grown in a wide variety of garden conditions and used to decorate many garden styles. They are a natural addition to the rock garden, when they are allowed to dry out and rest for the summer months. If naturalized in turf areas, delay the first grass mowing until the bulb leaves start to wither. Particularly well suited to growing under deciduous shrubs and trees, crocus bloom and obtain enough sunlight for continued existence before the larger plants leaf out, shading the bulbs for the summer. Once leafed out and growing, deciduous shrubs are efficient water collectors, removing the available water from the soil so the crocus bulbs are allowed to happily bake all summer in their dormant state.

Sometimes, wild, or species, crocus are available in bulb catalogs, and you might be tempted to indulge. If you have the proper place, such as a rock garden or small bed not dominated by perennials, then take a chance on planting a few different species of crocus. They are charming, easy-growing plants that will multiply and spread if they like their location. Although crocus in the wild are found in three different states of dry and wet conditions, the crocus commonly found in garden centers and catalogs can be grouped according to only two distinct sets of cultural requirements.

The first group includes hybrids of *C. chrysanthus* and the large-flowered Dutch hybrids. These bulbs require the dry conditions of summer dormancy to thrive. I have several groups of these scattered in rough rocky areas under maple trees at the end of my driveway, and they grow quite nicely with their summer baking. The second group is made up of hybrids of *C. vernus*. These flower much better if grown under constant moisture conditions. The *C. vernus* hybrids are wonderful pond-side bulbs, helping to launch the water garden into spring.

C. chrysanthus

Height: 2–5 inches

Bloom Time: Fourth week of April in zone 4

Depth to Plant: 2–3 inches

Spacing: 3–4 inches

Best Season to Plant: Fall

Sunlight Needed: Full sun

Crocus chrysanthus 'Jeanne d'Arc'

C. chrysanthus hybrids usually bloom in my garden about the first week of May. They are not the earliest bulb—some of the tiny species bulbs in the rock garden claim that honor—but they are one of the showiest of the small bulbs. *C. chrysanthus* hybrids come in a wide range of colors, from 'Remembrance', with its deep, dark violet petals, to 'Elegance', with its two-toned petals—a deep violet outer coloring enclosing a lemon yellow inner. They come in yellows and white, too, such as 'Goldilocks' and 'Purity'. In my gardens, I have found that the violet and deeper-colored bulbs last for many years. For some strange reason, it seems the birds like to peck away at the yellow-flowering crocus, and those bulbs disappear in 1 or 2 years. This is a personal tragedy, as I like the yellow-flowering varieties much more than the deeper purples. Another personal observation from my garden is that established crocus clumps bloom earlier than first-year plantings. So establishing a flowering plan based only on the first year's flowering results is difficult; count on established bulbs to bloom at least 5 days earlier than newly planted ones.

Large-Flowering Hybrids

Height: 5 inches
Bloom Time: Fourth week of April in zone 4
Depth to Plant: 2–3 inches
Spacing: 3–4 inches
Best Season to Plant: Fall
Sunlight Needed: Full sun

The large-flowering Dutch hybrids are the result of many years of hybridization, which focused on creating a larger bloom than the original species. Dutch hybrids are noted here because they are not only commonly found in retail areas but also make an excellent bulb for spring forcing. (Directions for forcing bulbs are found in Part Six.) Another reason for collecting these bulbs is that the large-flowering hybrids tend to flower a week later than the *C. chrysanthus* hybrids. Using a mix of these two crocus can create an extended bloom time in the garden. They do not respond all that well to sudden freezing weather after they have begun blooming. A surprise cold snap will shorten the bloom time drastically.

C. vernus

Height: 5 inches
Bloom Time: Fourth week of April in zone 4
Depth to Plant: 3–4 inches
Spacing: 3–4 inches
Best Season to Plant: Fall
Sunlight Needed: Full sun

The late-blooming *C. vernus* hybrids tend to have larger flowers than the *C. chrysanthus* varieties and, as noted, do much better in a general garden situation in which they are watered and fed all summer long. They like to be planted slightly deeper than other crocus; but this is not a major point, because the bulb will work its way to the proper depth with no assistance from us. The color range is similar to the large-flowering hybrids; cultivars include 'Yellow Mammoth' and 'Queen of the Blues'.

Eranthis hyemalis

Winter Aconite
Height: 3 inches
Bloom Time: Third to fourth week of April in zone 4
Depth to Plant: 4–5 inches
Spacing: 2–4 inches
Best Season to Plant: Fall
Sunlight Needed: Full sun to part shade

Eranthis hyemalis

The genus *Eranthis* was named from the Greek *er,* meaning "spring," and *anthos,* meaning "a flower." This is in fact a very early flowering spring bulb. A yellow charmer that earns its keep, winter aconite does have a few quirks the beginning gardener would do well to examine. This bulb does not like to dry out and really does prefer cool temperatures to hot, scorching days. In northern sunny gardens, the bulb will likely perform better if given a bit of shade instead of baking in the sun. The bulbs are small and do not resemble our common concept of a bulb; they look more like a piece of tree bark than a tulip bulb. But if they look dried out and dead looking in the sales shop, that is probably what they are. Good nurseries keep these bulbs packed cool and moist. Before planting them, it is an excellent idea to soak winter aconite bulbs for 24 hours in a tub of lukewarm water. The soaking revitalizes them, assisting in their establishment process. Although they prefer to stay damp, winter aconite bulbs do not like to be grown in swamps or clay soils. Quite the contrary; they prefer good drainage and an organic soil capable of holding good water reserves without drowning the bulb. *Eranthis* grows quite well under deciduous trees and shrubs and will thrive in these conditions in hot areas.

Erythronium

Dog-Tooth Violet, Trout Lily
Height: 8–10 inches
Bloom Time: First to second week of May in zone 4
Depth to Plant: 4 inches
Spacing: 3–5 inches
Best Season to Plant: Fall
Sunlight Needed: Shady, woodland areas

Erythronium dens-canis

Primarily a North American species, dog-tooth violet is a great shade-loving spring bloomer. Falling in love with this bulb is quite possible once you have seen it gracing a woodland garden. Where traditional bulbs fail in the shade, this plant excels. The genus name *Erythronium* comes from the Greek *erythros,* meaning "red"; the common name *dog-tooth violet* comes from the shape of the bulb, which resembles . . . well, a dog's big canine tooth. (*dens-canis* is horticultural Latin for "dog's tooth.") Although specialist growers have species of this plant suited to the rock garden, the plants offered by garden centers and catalogs are suited for a shady garden with good soil and adequate moisture.

Do not allow these bulbs to sit and dry out for long periods of time. Plant them as soon after receiving them as possible. Mix compost into the soil at planting, at least 1 shovelful for every 3 shovelsful of soil backfilled into the planting hole, or 1 to 2 pounds per square foot spread over the surface. Mulch well to preserve soil moisture and to create an even summer temperature. The best mulch is old chopped-up leaves; renew the mulch annually. Even soil moisture and temperature will produce an excellent show of bloom, as the bulb will thrive under these conditions. *E. dens-canis* is the most common species, and it now comes in a range of colors from whites, pinks through plums, and lavenders. The interesting colors are mostly available in mixes, although some specialty growers do identify colored cultivars by name. Three common cultivars are: 'Lilac Wonder', a medium lilac; 'White Purple King', a deep purple with a white center; and 'White Splendour', clear white.

Two hybrid *Erythronium* plants, which are crosses between *E. revolutum* and *E. tuolumnense,* may sometimes by found: 'Kondo' and 'Pagoda'. 'Kondo' has a bright yellow flower with brown rings; its leaves have multiple bronze spots. 'Pagoda' is a mellow golden yellow; its leaves

Erythronium 'Pagoda'

have so many bronze spots that they sometimes looks bronze with green spots rather than the reverse. Both, if they can be found, are excellent growing plants.

Fritillaria

Fritillary

Fritillary is a plant that requires a press agent. It has two strikes against it before it gets into the garden. The first is that its genus name comes from the Latin word *frittilus,* meaning "dice box." Apparently, the spotted flowers of *F. meleagris* reminded someone of a board for a dice game. Although this may not be of importance to some gardeners, the fact that most of the flowers of the *Fritillaria* genus smell like a skunk-works rather than a flower patch is sure to banish it from some gardens. You don't need to stand upwind from these flowers, but sticking your nose into the blossom isn't a recommended garden activity. However, we all do it at least once to see if the plant really does stink (it does!). Some garden catalogs sell this plant as a mole deterrent, advising that moles like the smell even less than we do. Although I cannot vouch for this, I can say that fritillary makes a delightful addition to the spring rock garden or the semishady bulb garden. Fritillary likes a spot where its summer dormancy is dryish, not bone dry as with the truly alpine bulbs, but in a spot where some water will be available from rainfall. Well-drained soil is a prerequisite for this bulb, so clay soils are out. The common species, such as *F. imperialis, F. meleagris,* and *F. michailovskyi,* all perform well if they are given moderately fertile soils and moderate summer moisture. They grow well at the front of the perennial border, as long as they are not shaded out too early before their leaves ripen and go dormant.

F. imperialis

Height: 3 feet

Bloom Time: Fourth week of May in zone 4

Depth to Plant: 6 inches

Spacing: 12 inches

Best Season to Plant: Middle to late fall

Sunlight Needed: Full sun

Fritillaria imperialis 'Lutea'

Crown imperial is one of the showiest of the *Fritillaria* species, but its bulb has a particular characteristic that beginner gardeners must be aware of. If you examine the bulb, you'll see a hollow section toward the top. If the bulb is planted in a spot where spring water collects, it is possible the water will sit inside the bulb, rotting it. To prevent this, plant this fritillary bulb on its side. The leaves will go up to the surface, and the bulb will not act as a water tub. The bulb may eventually pull itself upright as the roots establish their proper relationship to gravity. If crown imperial is placed in a garden that remains moister than this plant's natural habitat, it may be lost to rot after a few years. Crown imperial is a tall plant, with its 3-foot-high spikes, suited for the general perennial border. This is one flower that most gardeners will willingly smell only once. Native to Turkey, it comes in a variety of colors, ranging from the orange-yellow 'Lutea' to purple-and-orange 'The Premier'.

F. meleagris

Height: 2 inches–3 feet
Bloom Time: Third to fourth week of May in zone 4
Depth to Plant: 2–6 inches; small bulbs shallow, large bulbs deep
Spacing: 8–12 inches
Best Season to Plant: Middle to late fall
Sunlight Needed: Full sun to part shade

Sometimes *F. meleagris,* one of the most common fritillaries, can be diffi-cult to grow. It seems to pick and choose where it will survive on a random basis. If this bulb has disappeared in your garden, try planting it with lime mixed into the soil; and mulch with a lime-based rock, such as oyster shell grit (available at farm feed stores) or lime-based bird grit (available from pet stores). Never use peat moss or granite grit around a fritillary, as these amendments increase soil acidity. *F. meleagris* is a delightful plant in the general garden, growing between 12 and 18 inches tall. It is sold in a vari-ety of colors and named forms, but most have a checkered or spotted appearance. 'Charon', for example, is a dark purple and 'Aphrodite', as might be expected, is a clear white. *F. meleagris* is one fritillary species that will survive nicely in dappled shade.

F. michailovskyi

Height: 8 inches
Bloom Time: Third to fourth week of May in zone 4
Depth to Plant: 2–4 inches
Spacing: 3–4 inches
Best Season to Plant: Middle to late fall
Sunlight Needed: Full sun to part shade

If we ignore the pronunciation of this Turkish native for a few moments, we will find a delightful plant for the front of the border or rock garden. Reaching up to 8 inches in height (taller in shade than in sun), *F. michailovskyi* is easily grown and should be planted where it

Fritillaria michailovskyi

gets sun all day, good drainage, and summer heat (but not baked soil). I have some of these in my bulb rock garden right next to a huge boulder. The movement of the sun and the nearness of the large rock give it plenty of spring heat. It delights us every spring with its yellowish purple blooms and disappears near the end of June for its rest.

F. pontica

Height: 12–16 inches
Bloom Time: Third to fourth week of May in zone 4
Depth to Plant: 4 inches
Spacing: 4–6 inches
Best Season to Plant: Middle to late fall
Sunlight Needed: Full sun to part shade

I have noticed that *F. pontica* is starting to be offered in mail-order catalogs. This fritillary will do fine in a semishady garden. This native of Turkey and northern Greece enjoys a bit of summer water and fertile soil. At 12 to 16 inches tall, it is a good plant for the front of a perennial border but not farther back; it is not overly showy and easy to grow. The flowers are a light shade of green, often mottled with a touch of white. Because it's unique, this is exactly the kind of plant you put in the garden to show off to your neighbor; but that is the only reason you should be tempted. If happy, it will self-sow, and you'll have so many you may need to thin them out!

Galanthus nivalis

Snowdrop

Height: 4–6 inches
Bloom Time: First to second week May in zone 4
Depth to Plant: 3 inches
Spacing: 3–4 inches
Best Season to Plant: Fall or right after blooming
Sunlight Needed: Dappled shade

There are 20 species and hundreds of cultivars of snowdrops, a popular spring-blooming bulb. For the record, a cultivar is a form of a plant that is unique from other closely related forms. It is possible to breed a plant with the important leaf and other genetic characteristics of a particular species but with a different flower form. Snowdrops are available in hundreds of different flower forms, most of which are generally important only to collectors. The genus name—from the Greek *gala,* meaning "milk," and *anthos,* meaning "flower"—sums up the dominant color; although there are forms with varying amounts of green markings and shades of white ranging from clear crystal white to soft cream. Snowdrops are very easy to grow, and clumps will happily multiply in a garden that has cool winters. Gardeners in areas with warm winters will find this a difficult plant to grow.

Galanthus nivalis

Cultivars of *G. nivalis* are the ones most often found in catalogs, although other species are available through specialist bulb growers. The differences are mostly in flower form rather than in color; and unless you're a galanthophile, *G. nivalis* offers quite enough variety. From fully double flowers to singles in all forms of upright through nodding flowers, the common snowdrop will adorn any shady garden. It blooms 1 or 2 weeks later in cool shady gardens (because it takes a while to get the frost out of the ground in these areas) than in open sunny areas. To really make this bulb produce, mulch it with compost or leaf mold annually. The even temperature and moisture under the mulch, not to mention the decomposing nutrients, will produce bumper crops.

Hyacinthus orientalis

Hyacinth, Dutch Hyacinth

Height: 12 inches

Bloom Time: Third to fourth week of May in zone 4

Depth to Plant: 4 inches

Spacing: 4–6 inches

Best Season to Plant: Fall

Sunlight Needed: Full sun

Hyacinth enjoys warm summer dormancy. This means it should be given a garden spot that has good drainage and very little water during the summer months. It enjoys full sun and moderately fertile soil. After blooming, allow the leaves to dry out naturally and go dormant, as with all spring-blooming bulbs.

Hyacinthus orientalis 'Amethyst'

H. orientalis is the parent plant for the huge variety of hybrid hyacinth bulbs that grace garden center shelves every fall. Although it originally had a pale blue or violet flower, breeders have now developed a full range of colors, including the cultivars 'Amethyst', with a lilac bloom; 'Anna Marie', with a pink bloom; and 'Jan Bos', a bloodred bloom. Hyacinths are also available in a full range of blues and violets.

I have had only marginal success with hyacinths in my garden. I originally grew them in the main perennial border; but they died out within 2 years, largely I suspect, as a result of being overwatered during the summer. The water required by the main border perennials in our sandy soils was simply too much for the bulbs.

This bulb requires that you keep a sharp eye out for diseases. The common fungus botrytis attacks it with a vengeance, as do other problems, such as black slime and rhizoctonia (see "Problem Solving" on page 38 for more information). In all cases, if rotting foliage is seen, spray immediately with garden fungicides. Prune all spring foliage after it fades, and remove it

Hyacinthus orientalis 'Jan Bos'

from the garden. Do not compost the foliage. Prompt removal of dead or over-the-hill flowers will also reduce fungal attacks. This warning is not meant to deter you from growing hyacinths; rather it is meant as a reminder that a bit of extra vigilance is needed to continue to enjoy its beauty.

Definitely plant hyacinths in clumps. The more in the clump, the better it will look. At the absolute minimum, use 3–5 bulbs in a single spot and of any one variety; otherwise hyacinths look lonely and lost in the spring.

Hyacinthoides

Bluebell

Height: 12–20 inches
Bloom Time: First to second week of May in zone 4
Depth to Plant: 2–3 inches
Spacing: 2–4 inches
Best Season to Plant: Fall
Sunlight Needed: Shade to part shade

Be careful with bluebell: If it's happy in its location, it will spread vigorously, giving the gardener enough new bulbs to supply the entire neighborhood, town, or perhaps even the city.

Hyacinthoides hispanica

It is a wonderful spring bulb, but it can become a bit of a pest. It tends to rapidly colonize fertile, damp (but not sopping) areas under the shade of deciduous trees. Gardening legends say it prefers oak trees to any other; but given the right conditions, I don't think it will be too fussy.

Bluebells are fragrant; so wandering in a colonized area, on a still May evening, just before the mosquitoes come out, can be a heady experience. The bulbs can be readily moved right after flowering or in the fall; however, they will be much deeper in the ground than the size of their flowers suggests. Digging down 6–8 inches should get most bulbs. This is one plant that seems to decide independently where it will grow. There are reports of it growing on clay soils as well as sandy soils; so if you have a bit of clay in your garden, you might find it a useful bulb. Bluebells will not spread as fast in clay as they will in a more open, better-drained soil. The flowers are much better looking in the shade or dappled shade than they are in full sun. The plants grow well in full sun; but the colors of the blooms looked bleached out, making them less attractive.

There are two species in cultivation: *H. non-scripta* and *H. hispanica.* They cross-pollinate like mad, so no matter what you start with, very quickly flowers will determine their own forms. Interestingly enough, it may be necessary to search for this bulb in North America. Being a bit of a weed in Europe, it is not often offered in catalogs. If you can get some from a neighbor, do so.

Iris (Bulbous)

Bulbous Iris

Of the more than 200 species of *Iris,* all have fibrous root systems and some form of storage organs in the form of bulbs or rhizomes. Many of the bulbous iris are normally delightful spring bloomers. The plants that use rhizomes for food storage tend to bloom in early summer and will be described in Part Four.

The bulbous iris are a bit particular about where and how they are placed in the garden, so success with these bulbs is more demanding than with most other bulbs. The delight of seeing the blooms in the early spring is worth the bit of trouble they take. In contrast, some of the summer-blooming rhizomatous iris are among the easiest of garden plants, if some simple conditions are met.

Many times catalogs describe bulbous iris as easy, leading the reader to blithely purchase and plant these gems. The truth in my garden is that they are rather more demanding than many other bulbs. Throughout these plant portraits, the words *summer dry* come up repeatedly; and although many bulbs want dry conditions, they rarely demand them—struggling along with some water. Bulbous iris are serious about this condition if long-term success is desired. Getting the bulbs to flower the first year after planting is relatively easy; it is much more difficult to keep them happy in successive years.

Iris do best in climates where the winters are cold and dry and the summers are warm and dry. Surrounding the dry winter and summer with a damp spring and fall is acceptable to the bulb, but summer damp will cause one of several things to happen. Moisture, collecting on unripened foliage and sliding down toward the bulb, rots the bulb before it has a chance to ripen and go dormant. Sometimes, if it does not rot under excess moisture, the bulb simply divides itself into multiple tiny bulbs that then never do anything in the garden, except rot in subsequent years. Gardeners living in warmer or damper maritime climates can either shelter iris from the elements with panes of glass or grow them in pots in greenhouses. Growing them in the ground in these areas is tough and not for beginners. Northern gardeners will have more success than southerners with these bulbs, because of the freezing conditions and lack of available water during the winter months.

Summer care is as easy as planting them in alpine or rock gardens under the eaves of houses or next to the driveway where the water will not collect or stay long.

Having given you a warning, I must say that iris are gorgeous; and visitors to my spring garden never fail to spy them out and ask about them. It is all I can do to convince my wife that she should not take them as cut flowers for the house; because like their taller bearded cousins, they make excellent cut flowers.

One of the delights of iris is that they are true to their namesake. The plants were named after Iris, the Greek goddess of the rainbow. In Greek mythology, she was a messenger of Zeus and left Mount Olympus only to convey commands to humans. She was portrayed as a beautiful maiden with multicolored wings and clothing and, because of her rapid speed in the sky, was always trailed by a rainbow. Iris do indeed come in a bewildering variety of colors, and choosing which to grow will take as much time as actually growing them.

I. danfordiae

Height: 4–6 inches
Bloom Time: Second week of May in zone 4
Depth to Plant: 2–4 inches
Spacing: 4 inches
Best Season to Plant: Fall
Sunlight Needed: Full sun

Iris danfordiae

I give this species of bulbous iris its own description because it is often offered separately from the *I. reticulata* species to which it more properly belongs. This bulb has the well-deserved reputation of disappearing into multiple tiny bulblets at the hint of stress. It is a bulb that thrives on summer neglect, heat, and total absence of water; without these appalling garden conditions, it will perish. My original planting of them survived 2 years in an alpine bulb garden. I believe they perished during a drought when I watered the rock garden to preserve some wilting plants. Having realized the folly of this combination, I put the next planting of these iris in a more innovative location, which was dug with a pickax rather than a shovel. This second planting has done well, because it is planted in the hard-packed gravel of the farm's driveway right next to the bulb garden. Although protected from traffic, the iris are in an area that resists water penetration, so most rain runs away from this spot and it dries out early in the spring.

The second thing I did to keep these bulbs alive and thriving was to plant them much deeper than normally recommended. Instead of placing the bulbs 2 inches deep, I put them 4–6 inches down. Again, this reduces the amount of surface water they will obtain. Now the bulbs seem happy for the moment and brighten up the spring with their Turkish yellow blossoms.

I. hollandica

Dutch Iris

Height: 4–6 inches

Bloom Time: Second week of May in zone 4

Depth to Plant: 2–4 inches

Spacing: 4 inches

Best Season to Plant: Fall

Sunlight Needed: Full sun

Iris × hollandica 'Blue Magic'

Dutch iris are often offered in catalogs, and their appealing pictures entice and enthrall unwary gardeners. The catalogs tend to say that these iris are hardy in all but the most severe of winters. Well, I can tell you that my zone 4 garden is too severe, because I have not yet been able to winter them. Catalogs do not agree with me, but the Holland Flower Bulb Resource people have identified Dutch iris as doing best in the warmer areas of North America, down into zone 8. The warmth seems to be more critical than the summer drying for these plants, although good drainage is a necessity. This is a bulb for adventurous northern gardeners or for anyone living in warmer areas. The color range is complete from the boldest yellows of 'Royal Yellow' to the violets of 'Blue Magic'.

I. reticulata

Height: 4–6 inches

Bloom Time: Second week of May in zone 4

Depth to Plant: 2–4 inches

Spacing: 4 inches

Best Season to Plant: Fall

Sunlight Needed: Full sun

I. reticulata are commonly offered in catalogs without any description of their specific needs. If these iris are grown in exactly the same way as described for *I. danfordiae* (page 67), then success is ensured, or at least possible. Straying from the winter and summer dry conditions will cause bulb death. *I. reticulata* comes in a full range of blue and violet cultivars for the spring palette: 'Harmony' is the color of a blue-bird, 'Joyce' is a sky blue, and 'Purple Gem' is aptly named.

Iris reticulata 'Harmony'

As an aside, I suggest you plant these bulbs in the driest section of the garden, if for no other reason than to see them bloom the first year. If they survive to do so again then you are triumphant. That first year, those first blooms are worth all the anguish of losing them in subsequent years.

Juno Iris

Height: 4–6 inches
Bloom Time: Second week of May in zone 4
Depth to Plant: 2–4 inches
Spacing: 4 inches
Best Season to Plant: Fall
Sunlight Needed: Full sun

Juno iris are wonderful bloomers that are ideally suited to areas of the Southwest where summer rainfall is nonexistent and winter temperatures are cold. The only North American native iris in this class, *I. planifolia,* is found in the Southwest. The majority of this iris are found in the hot and dry summer areas of western Asia—Turkey to southern Russia—which tells us a bit about their requirements. Although Juno iris are not as demanding as *I. reticulata* and *I. danfordiae,* they will rot in the wet, cool summers of the north. If you are determined to try to grow these bulbs, try *I. aucheri, I. bucharica,* and *I. magnifica*; from gardeners' reports, they seem to be more tolerant of water.

I included the Juno iris here because they have very appealing flowers; and once seen in catalogs or on posters, they will demand a place in the heart and garden of most iris lovers. When growing Junos, be careful with the bulb; folklore has it that they do not appreciate having their roots disturbed or broken in transition from garden to garden. In practice, it is not too critical, but avoid excessively rough handling. Juno iris do appreciate spring moisture and a fertilizer that is heavy on the potash and phosphorus rather than nitrogen.

Leucojum

Spring snowflake, summer snowflake
Height: 20 inches
Bloom Time: First week of May in zone 4
Depth to Plant: 3–4 inches
Spacing: 4–6 inches—forms clumps
Best Season to Plant: Fall
Sunlight Needed: Part shade

Leucojum aestivum

Leucojum, an interesting word, is derived from Greek and is a general name for any white, fragrant flower. Summer snowflake (*L. aestivum*) is commonly available in catalogs and is the hardiest of the species. It is happiest in damp soils and semishaded areas. It will survive quite nicely in the regular garden soil of the mixed perennial border into zone 4, but it's not likely to make it much farther north. A spring bloomer (the common name is a misnomer), summer snowflake is spectacular in larger clumps next to a pond. Spring snowflake (*L. vernum*) is also readily available. It blooms in early spring, right alongside the bulbous iris in the last week of April or first week in May. It is not as hardy as *I. aestivum* and so is found in slightly warmer gardens from zone 5 south. It does share the love of damp ground and semishady spots, so plant it accordingly.

Muscari latifolium

Grape hyacinth

Height: 8–10 inches

Bloom Time: Second week of May in zone 4

Depth to Plant: 3–4 inches

Spacing: 6 inches

Best Season to Plant: Fall

Sunlight Needed: Full sun

Muscari latifolium

Grape hyacinth is one of the easiest and hardiest of bulbs. Given a full sun position with good drainage, they bloom without problems for years. If they are happy, they will multiply, and may require dividing if they get too crowded. If they require division (lots of leaves with few flowers is a symptom), simply dig up the clump in the fall, separate the bulbs and replant 2–3 inches apart. Clay soil or a wet spring garden spot will damage the bulbs; and neither they nor the gardener will be happy with the outcome.

There are many excellent cultivars and species of grape hyacinth offered in catalogs; and although none has huge flowers, when mass planted their blue-violet color makes a truly spectacular show. A minimum of 20 bulbs in each location will give a show; fewer than that are lonely. All types are easy to grow and worthwhile in the rock garden or front of the border. Choose the bulb based on the color (shades of blue through violets) that is desired in the garden. *Muscari* naturalize easily and will do well under deciduous trees, where they bloom and receive their quotient of spring light before the trees leaf out. If planted under trees, plant out at the drip line of the tree rather than close to the trunk for best growing results. Grape hyacinths can be double planted with tulips for some truly interesting results, but make sure the tulip selected will flower at the same time. If planted in the lawn, do not mow until the leaves have started to wither or mow with the blade deck in its highest position for the summer. (An excellent idea in any case for turf health.) Although these plants are dormant in the summer, they begin growth by leafing out in the fall, and their leaves remain green through the winter.

Narcissus

Daffodil

Height: 3–16 inches

Bloom Time: First week of May in zone 4; varies by type

Depth to Plant: 1¹/₂ times bulb depth

Spacing: 4–6 inches

Best Season to Plant: Fall

Sunlight Needed: Full sun to dappled shade

Although we all enjoy the spring jauntiness of *Narcissus,* the origin of the name refers to a characteristic of the bulb we would be well to remember. It comes from the Greek for "deep sleep or stupor." Readers will recognize the root word for *narcotic* in this definition. The name is a reference to an alkaloid contained within narcissus bulbs that if eaten in quantity can

Narcissus jonquilla 'Golden Perfection'

lead to stupor and paralysis. Luckily, reports have it that anybody eating a narcissus bulb would have to have dead taste buds, as it is an extremely foul-tasting bulb (I claim no culinary experience with narcissus), and even children will take no more than one small willing bite.

A distinction between daffodil and narcissus was originally made by cut-flower growers and bulb producers based on the length of the corona (the cup part of the flower). Flowering bulbs with long corona cups were called daffodils, and a short corona earned the flower the title of narcissus. With the amazing interbreeding taking place today, this distinction no longer holds true. Thus the natural wild-growing parent stocks are called narcissus, and the plants of indeterminate breeding used in our gardens are known as daffodils. Although garden daffodil flower forms are obviously based on the original parental narcissus flower, the flower shapes and often the coloring of daffodils are not normally found in the wild narcissus.

Planting Daffodil Bulbs

The daffodil is one bulb that will grow just about anywhere and brings a wonderful charm to the spring garden. Although it does prefer a soil that is moist but well drained for its growing period, it will successfully struggle through almost anything but swamp conditions. Its love for sunshine is clear, but its success under deciduous trees and shrubs creates legendary flower effects in bulb display gardens. Gardeners who live in extremely warm and dry climates will find that the late-flowering cultivars do much better when given dappled shade rather than allowing them to fry out in the middle of the garden. Some wild narcissus appreciate a drying-out period, but the garden daffodils do not, preferring instead a normally watered garden soil. Daffodils for the most part are quite hardy and will survive in all but the most northern gardens; however, they do appreciate a mulch. Apply the mulch, not for the winter survival benefits but to achieve the even temperature and moisture conditions under the mulch during the spring and summer growing periods. One delightful aspect of daffodil flowers that is different from other bulbs is that their leaves and flowers are quite frost hardy. In my gardens, I have a clump of crocus close to a clump of small cyclamineus daffodils. Late snows and heavy frosts will decimate the large Dutch hybrid crocus, shortening their bloom times drastically; but the daffodils rarely even acknowledge the problem.

Plant daffodil bulbs $1^1/_2$ times their depth. This is a rule of thumb that was made to be broken by adventurous gardeners or those with specific needs. Generally, a daffodil bulb that is planted deeper than this (to 8 inches) will establish more effectively and need less frequent division, because it takes longer to crowd itself out than one that is shallowly planted. Shallowly planted bulbs make new bulbs faster than the deeply planted ones, and their flowers are not as large as the more deeply planted ones. A deeper planting can then be left in the garden for a long time before it has to be dug up and divided. If deep-planted bulbs are placed 6 inches apart, 1–2 inches farther than normally recommended, you will get 1 or 2 extra years between divisions.

When clumps of daffodils become large yet produce few flowers, fertilizing or dividing is required. Oftentimes, liberal amounts of fertilizer spread over the planting area in the fall has dramatic effects on poorly flowering clumps. But if the fertilizer method fails, or you simply want to increase the size of your planting by dividing, then dig the clump up in the early fall, pull the bulbs apart with your hands (they are joined at their bases), and replant right away. You can also dig up and divide the bulbs in the spring just after the plants have flowered while the leaves are still green. No trade secrets here; it is quite easy, and the bulb patch will really expand when this is done, tripling in size at the very least. My own experience is that the daffodils in the garden clump up and require dividing more often than those planted in grass or left to naturalize. In naturalizing, the bulbs do not increase as quickly as they do in flower borders. The food and water available to the bulbs is much less, and the competition with other plants is greater. I have untouched clumps in the driveway wild gardens that date back 20 years to my first plantings.

There are only a few things to take into account when planting daffodils into turf for naturalizing. The first is the method of planting. I have used a bulb auger on the end of my electric drill quite successfully for most plantings, although it does chew up the grass quite severely. Old-fashioned bulb dibble planters create less damage in turf than do the augers. An alternative recommended in some manuals is to strip away the turf, rolling it up like a carpet; plant the bulbs; and then roll the turf back. I have never done this, because it seems like a lot of work; but if I had hundreds of bulbs to plant, this might be the solution. I find that sprinkling some peat moss, compost, and grass seed over the holes and damaged areas in the very early spring quickly fixes any problems caused by rambunctious planting sprees; but then again, I am not a lawn fanatic. Flower fanatic yes, lawn fanatic no.

One garden activity that must be taken into account when planting daffodils in turf is that the leaves of the bulbs must be left alone to feed and restore the bulb for next year's blooming before the lawn is mowed. Wait at least 4–6 weeks after flowering before mowing. Do not mow any lawn that has naturalized bulbs with less than a 2-inch deck height.

Feeding daffodil bulbs is quite easy. Feed the plants around them, and the bulbs will get the leftovers and thrive quite nicely. If you're determined to grow a super crop of daffodils, the use of formulations with extra potash (the third number on the fertilizer label) will pay dividends in flower formation for the bulbs as well as for the surrounding flowers and plants. Remember that an early spring feeding will not affect that year's flowering; you feed for this year's bulb growth and next year's flowering. Once the daffodil leaves have faded down, put annual plants over top of them; but do not cultivate so deeply as to nick the bulbs. Feed the annuals with a balanced plant food, and give them a shot of liquid food once a month through the growing season; this will ensure the daffodils stay healthy and happy for the following spring.

HOW NARCISSUS GOT ITS NAME

Narcissus, one of those Greeks specially favored by the gods, had been given the ability to stay young and beautiful for his entire life—provided that he never saw his own reflection. When he made the mistake of spurning the attentions of the nymph Echo, she convinced Nemesis, the goddess of retribution and vengeance, to help her with revenge. Versions disagree about how Narcissus was tricked into looking into a pool of water; but when he did, he was instantly frozen in place to regard his own reflection for eternity. Some storytellers feel pity for the poor tricked youth, seeing his fate as a metaphor for modern society; others portray him as a fitting role model for narcissistic behavior. Whatever the interpretation, the narcissus flower grew up beside the pond in memory of the great beauty of this Greek youth.

Flower Parts of the Daffodil

If you choose your bulb from a color picture in a catalog, the distinctions between the different daffodil divisions are not overly important; the picture lets you know what you'll receive. But if you order bulbs from mail-order suppliers, you'll want to refer to the descriptions given in "Daffodil Divisions" and the accompanying illustration on pages 76–77, so you'll know what the flower will look like. Note that the differences or relationships between the corona and the perianth distinguish the different daffodil divisions. The corona is the cup-shaped part of the bloom, and the perianth refers to the petals at the base of the cup.

DAFFODIL DIVISIONS

Division	Type	Flowers to a Stem	Characteristics
1	Trumpet daffodils	1	Corona as long as or longer than perianth segments
2	Large-cupped daffodils	1	Corona more than $1/3$ but less than equal to length of perianth segments
3	Small-cupped daffodils	1	Corona not more than $1/3$ length of perianth segments
4	Double daffodils	1 or more	Doubling of perianth segments or corona or both
5	Triandrus daffodils	2 or more	Perianth segments reflexed (pointing back); flower hanging
6	Cyclamineus daffodils	1 (usually)	Perianth segments reflexed; flower at acute angle to stem
7	Jonquilla daffodils	1–3	Perianth segments spreading, not reflexed; flowers fragrant; leaves narrow
8	Tazetta daffodils	3–20	Perianth segments spreading, not reflexed; flowers fragrant; leaves broad
9	Poeticus daffodils	1	Perianth segments pure white; disk-shaped corona with green or yellow center and reddish rim; flowers fragrant
10	Species, wild variants	1–20	All wild species, i.e., narcissus or unclassified reputed wild hybrids
11	Split-corona daffodils	1 (usually)	Corona split, not lobed, usually for more than half its length
12	Miscellaneous	Variable	Anything else not classified

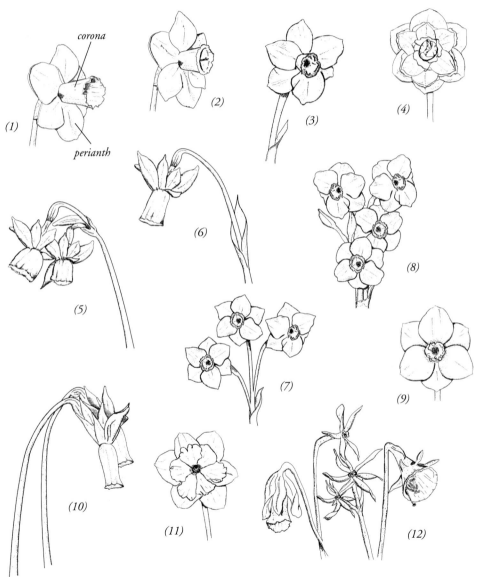

The number refers to the division, described in "Daffodil Divisions" on page 76.

A Final Thought on Narcissus

The wild species of *Narcissus* are not generally available, although there are some very interesting miscellaneous class plants being sold in specialist bulb catalogs. The specialist plants are no harder to grow than the larger more common daffodils; it is just that their flowers are not as showy. They are suited for the alpine or the naturalized rock garden rather than a perennial or house border; and it is the alpine gardener or specialist bulb grower who falls in love with them. If you are just starting with bulbs and small daffodils, by all means try them in these places, but not before experimenting with the hundreds of improved garden performers that are more easily available.

Ornithogalum

Star-of-Bethlehem

Star-of-Bethlehem has an interesting historical background. Derived from the Greek words *ornis,* meaning "bird," and *gala,* meaning "milk," the flowers are indeed white; the bird reference, however, is not so polite or mentionable in company. *Ornithogalum umbellatum* is thought to be the biblical plant referred to as dove's dung; a measure of these, known as a "cab," sold for a shekel during the Babylonian siege of Jerusalem. The common name Star-of-Bethlehem obviously refers to its star-shaped petals. The two hardiest bulbs normally sold as Star-of-Bethlehem are *O. nutans* and *O. umbellatum.*

O. nutans

Height: 6–8 inches
Bloom Time: Third week of May in zone 4
Depth to Plant: 2–3 inches
Spacing: 12–15 inches
Best Season to Plant: Fall
Sunlight Needed: Full sun to part shade

Known as either Star-of-Bethlehem or silver bell, this bulb is reliably hardy in zone 4 and has even naturalized (becoming a weed) in

Ornithogalum nutans

some parts of the Northeast. It is an excellent choice for the shady garden and will happily multiply from a limited planting. The major differences between this species and *O. umbellatum,* is that *O. nutans* is a few inches taller and has a broader green stripe on the back of the flower. *O. nutans* will likely do a bit better in deeper shade than will *O. umbellatum.* Otherwise, treat them the same.

O. umbellatum

Height: 6–8 inches
Bloom Time: Third week of May in zone 4
Depth to Plant: 2–3 inches
Spacing: 12–15 inches
Best Season to Plant: Fall
Sunlight Needed: Full sun to part shade

Ornithogalum umbellatum

Whether we call it dove's dung or star-of-Bethlehem, the commonly available *O. umbellatum* is easily grown. In fact, too easily grown. This bulb clumps into a good mass, and then spreads around the garden via seeds. Its tendency to wander and spread may account for its pejorative old common name. Star-of-Bethlehem seems particularly happy in the semishade under shrubs or along the edges of tree shade. So far, it has colonized various parts of my garden but has not yet hit the lawn. Other gardeners have told me that it likes the lawn as much as the garden; I am still waiting, although the reports bode well for a plan to naturalize these bulbs in a grass setting. I have allowed this bulb to wander around, picking its own sites, because I enjoy its glowing white cheerfulness in the spring. Each bulb will form into a cheerful 8–10-inch-wide clump in 2–3 years. It does come up a bit later than other species bulbs; but then again, it has chosen the shadier, cooler spots in the garden. Unfortunately, it has no fragrance to speak of.

There are several types of *Ornithogalum* that are not winter hardy in any but the warmest parts of North America. These African species can be treated as summer-flowering bulbs, planted in the spring and collected in the fall. They are not as easy as some of the other summer-flowering bulbs but can be tried by the adventurous.

Puschkinia scilloides

Striped squill

Height: 6 inches

Bloom Time: Fourth week of April in zone 4

Depth to Plant: 2 inches

Spacing: 2–4 inches

Best Season to Plant: Fall

Sunlight Needed: Full sun to light shade

Puschkinia scilloides var. *libanotica*

Striped squill is native to the Caucasus Mountains, Turkey, and northern Iran. These delightful little bulbs were originally described by Count Mussin-Puschkin, a Russian chemist who was collecting plants for herbarium use. These plants display a grouping of star-shaped flowers that are among the earliest in the spring bulb bed. The flowers range from a light blue to white with a distinctive darker stripe down the middle; they are particularly attractive when massed in large clumps. They handle late snows or frost with no difficulty; in fact, this is an almost trouble-free, pest-free bulb. Plant it and watch it grow. Because of its size, it is an excellent bulb for the naturalized grass bed or in the rock garden. Striped squill will tend to get lost in the main perennial border but will make an attractive clump when planted just under the edge of deciduous shrubs. Commonly available, *Puschkinia* is an inexpensive bulb. Its low cost enables us to plant them in large clumps for maximum show.

Scilla

Scilla

Height: 3–5 inches

Bloom Time: Third to fourth week of May in zone 4

Depth to Plant: 2 inches

Spacing: 2–4 inches

Best Season to Plant: Fall

Sunlight Needed: Very shade tolerant

Taxonomists have been using *scilla* to have a good time confusing ordinary gardeners. The Greek word *skilla,* meaning "quill," was originally used to name the plant *Urginea maritima.* Based on a similar leaf shape, the familiar English bluebell (*S. nutans*) was also placed in the genus *Scilla* and received the common names of scilla and bluebell, depending on the reference. Now, to confuse the issue, the English bluebell scilla (*S. nutans*) was renamed *Hyacinthoides* (see page 64) and is now called *Hyacinthoides non-scripta* by horticulturists. *Urginea* is also no longer classed as or called scilla, which may be a relief to this tender African bulb, which is treated as a summer bulb in anything colder than zone 8 or 9. So the original bulbs of this genus are no longer called *Scilla.*

Scilla 'Alba'

This leaves us with the other bulbs that were also classified as *Scilla* and lumped into this category. Luckily, there is a scilla for almost every hardiness rating, and they are wonderful little spring bloomers for the rock garden or shady naturalized garden. Liking shade, they do very well planted beneath shrubs or trees and, if happy, will quickly form colonies. Requiring almost no care or attention once planted, scilla are an essential part of almost every shade bulb garden. They are, for the most part, hardy between zones 3 and 8. *S. sibirica* is among the hardiest to bloom, and it is commonly available in two colors: 'Spring Beauty' is a dark blue, and 'Alba' is a clear white. Through discussions with other gardeners in various parts of North America, I have learned that the spreading nature of the *Scilla* genus is very much connected to the warmth of the climate. In zone 4, where I live, *S. scilloides* rarely produces more than a

Scilla 'Spring Beauty'

compact clump of easily managed flowers; in zone 7 it is a rampant pest, overwhelming gardens with no compunction or regret. *S. peruviana*, as its name suggests, is quite tender; and although wonderful in zones 7–9, it survives only as a potted plant in any colder area. Read catalog descriptions carefully to find the plant that is suited for your hardiness zone. The performance of scilla varies widely by type.

Tulipa

Tulip

Tulips are easily the most popular of spring bulbs. Their trouble-free habits and ease of cultivation endear them to beginners and experts alike. Donating any space in a bulb book to them seems almost superfluous, because we all know the bulbs, we know the stories about tulip-o-mania and the fact that some poor fellow in medieval Holland paid kitchen chairs, wagons, oxen,

A tulip field in Holland.

geese, and a fantastic amount of gold for a single bulb. If you have grown bulbs, the odds are that you have grown tulips. Although familiarity may sometimes breed contempt, it does not do so for me and my tulips. The longer I grow tulips, the more I come to enjoy them, their forms, and their color range. While I grow mostly early tulips in my main perennial borders, some smaller tulips are even finding their way into my rock gardens. These species tulips are wonderful little gems that are offered through specialty catalogs and are generally no harder to grow than the larger garden hybrids. Some are even starting to self-sow, making a nuisance of themselves between the other plants and rocks.

Although we can still identify the smaller plants botanically (*T. tarda*, for example), identifying the genetic parentage of the main garden tulips is not that easy. With the hybridization that has been going on for 600 years, the original parentage is now a source of debate for botanists and geneticists. When these debates begin to rage, those of us who garden merely smile and go back to planting. Whatever the parentage and whatever the genes, these are wonderful plants for the spring garden.

Planting and Growing Tulips

There are two basic ways to grow tulip bulbs. Traditionally, tulips are planted 2–3 inches deep in October, and their flowers are enjoyed the following spring. The tulips then are allowed to grow until the leaves have soaked up enough sunshine, completed their growth cycle, and withered away. Once the tulips' leaves have died, a gardener who is growing tulips in the traditional style digs up the bulbs; allows them to air dry until the soil clinging to the roots is dry; and cleans them of soil, dead foliage, and old roots. The bulbs are taken indoors and stored in a cool, dry spot for the summer. In October, the traditional gardener replants the bulbs so the cycle can be repeated the following year. This annual digging and handling was reputed for years to keep the bulbs in prime condition and ensure a proper rest and recovery for subsequent blooming years. Gardeners do this because they believe the bulbs are healthier, will survive longer, and will flower more profusely than if the bulb were left in place for several years or more. In fact, modern research suggests that this may not be the best way to handle tulips; the following method is better.

Nontraditional gardeners left the tulip bulbs in the place where they were planted. I have a genetic predisposition to easy gardening and leave my tulips in the ground rather than endure the work of digging them up every summer. Tulips have a genetic predisposition to hot, dry summers and dry soils once their initial spring bloom and growth have finished. The bulbs prefer summer dryness to damp. If the garden is kept well watered for annual plant growth or the ground is a clay soil with subsequent poor drainage, the bulbs will not be happy. Having said that, I leave my garden tulips in place and have for many years. Fed well and allowed full spring growth without interference with the leaves, my tulips have continued to bloom quite successfully. There may be losses, but no more or less than can be expected from other perennial garden plants. Most of the losses seem to happen in the first or second year; once the tulips have settled in, they go for years with little extra care.

How should you plant your tulips? Other garden manuals will describe a planting depth of 2–3 inches for traditional planting but in my gardens, I plant them 8–12 inches deep and 3–4 inches apart for three reasons. The first is so the squirrels and chipmunks do not dig them up and have lunch at my garden's expense. The second is that deep planting allows me to grow annuals and perennials over top of the bulbs. This gives a full-season flower show in the same garden space. The third is that the bulb auger on the end of my electric drill easily reaches this depth, and any shallower than 3 inches causes the nearby planting holes to collapse into each other before I can get a bulb into them. Deep planting puts the bulb down out of sight and out of mind for the main summer months. The odd ones that disappear every year because of cultivation damage or other causes are simply replaced in the fall. The flower lover in me says that these odd losses not only give me a chance to increase the number of tulips I am growing but also allow me to obtain some new colors and hybrids. By regularly planting bulbs every year, whether it is necessary or not, a marvelous spring showing is ensured, and the bulb beds get larger and larger. There is always room for a new tulip or two . . . or three.

Design Tips

Flower bed designing is a matter of individual taste, but creating a strong visual impact is easier if a few good rules of thumb are followed. To begin with, plant at least a dozen bulbs in a single clump. A dozen is the minimum number to create any sense of impact; fewer and the bulbs look lonely and lost. I prefer clumps of 25 or more in my own garden. Stick to a single color in the clump. Although it is an acceptable idea to mix colors in the garden, planting each color by itself will give a much more dramatic impact than mixing all the colors together. Have clumps of different colors in the garden, rather than mixed color clumps. Never line up the tulips in a single row so they resemble toy soldiers on parade. All that is needed to reduce this toy soldier row to shambles is a nocturnal visit by a chipmunk and the line is 1 or 2 (or more!) soldiers short. If a formal bed is desired and straight rows are part of that design, plant enough bulbs to achieve a complete carpet. If this restricts the plant budget, do one of two things: Concentrate the available bulbs in one spot for maximum impact or do what most gardeners do and increase the plant budget. Plant too many tulips rather than too few. Too few of anything looks lonely; and if one or two bulbs die or do not produce flowers, the effect on a large planting will be minimal but the effect on a small planting can be devastating.

Feeding Tips

Feed the leaves and not the flowers. For tulips this advice is important if the bulbs are to continue blooming every year. Although they're not heavy feeders, tulips do require adequate feeding if they are to maintain their size and flowering potential. Before the use of chemical fertilizers, compost was added quite heavily to the Dutch bulb growing fields for a daffodil crop; the following year, one crop of tulips could be grown on the same field without additional feeding. If the garden above the tulip bulbs is fed with compost at 2–4 pounds per square foot, no other specific bulb food is necessary. If, instead, a balanced plant food (either granular or liquid) is used to grow the perennials and annuals above the bulbs, enough will filter down to help the bulbs. If the gardener chooses not to feed the plants above the tulips, then the bulbs will slowly wear down and flowering will stop. It may take 1 or 2 years of good feeding to bring them back into flowering after several years of neglect.

Some authors recommend dropping fertilizer into the hole when planting the bulbs, but this is not something I practice or recommend. If the overall soil condition is healthy because of the continued application of compost, extra fertilizer is unnecessary. When plant food is put beside emerging tender roots, there is a distinct possibility that the fertilizer will burn the roots. If you feel an irresistible urge to put something into the hole when planting, try bone meal. This is your safest choice; it will not burn the roots and might do some good.

Long-Term Care

Parallel to the advice for feeding tulips, it's important to grow the foliage, not the flower. Tulips throw several small leaves, and then they shove up this gorgeous flower stalk for our enjoyment. Once the flower is finished, prune the flower stalk to prevent the bulb from setting seed, because it takes energy to set seed. As gardeners we want our bulbs to use their energy to maintain or increase their own size and flowering strength, not set seed.

The single most important thing a tulip grower can do is to allow the leaves to remain undisturbed in the garden until they fade and begin to wither away. The temptation is to cut the foliage back right away or to tie it up in a ball over the top of the plant so you can plant your annuals in the same bed. This is especially true in a late spring when the garden includes late-flowering tulips. You want to get the annuals in and growing or they will not amount to anything by midsummer, but those silly bulb leaves are still growing away, taking up good garden space. If those "silly" bulb leaves are cut off or prevented from doing their work in any way, they won't be able to replace the energy used by the bulb when it produced the flower. Therefore, in several years, after a very wet summer or cold winter, the stressed tulip will come up blind, producing no flower, or worse yet it will simply disappear from the garden. Because the leaves produced a reduced amount of stored energy, the bulbs themselves will slowly decline. Planting tulips in too much shade results in the same effect. If the bulb cannot get enough energy, it will decline.

It cannot be repeated enough that the best thing a gardener can do for tulips is to allow the leaves to grow undisturbed until they begin to wither. If the bulbs in your garden bloom a bit late in the season and the annual garden is waiting, simply replace the existing bulbs with earlier varieties. Or add some earlier and later tulips along with a variety of summer- and fall-flowering bulbs and create a wonderful bulbs-only bed.

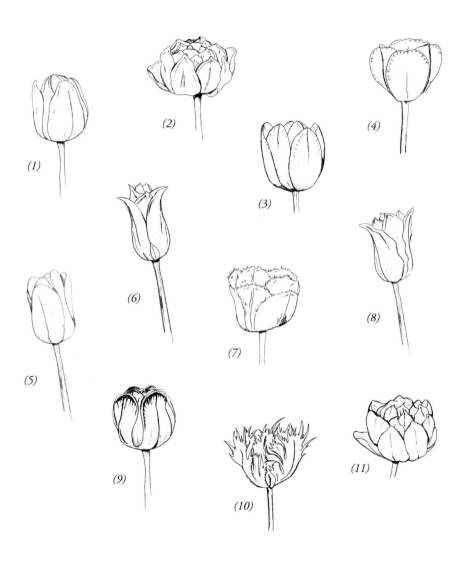

Some of the different kinds of garden tulips: (1) single early, (2) double early, (3) triumph, (4) Darwin hybrid, (5) single late, (6) lily-flowered, (7) fringed, (8) viridiflora, (9) Rembrandt, (10) parrot, (11) double late or peony-flowered.

Single Early Tulips

Height: 12–16 inches

Flower Size: 3–5 inches

Bloom Time: First to second week of May in zone 4

Planting Depth: 3 inches or 8–12 inches for rodent protection

Spacing: 2–4 inches

Planting Time: Fall, best after September

Sunlight Needed: Full sun

Tulipa 'Princess Irene' (single early)

Single early tulips have a special spot in the garden because they can easily be used as underplantings for other perennial plants. I use these tulips in my main perennial border. By the time the perennials are growing tall enough to shade the tulip foliage, the foliage has begun to die back. I planted them in clumps both at the front of and at the back of the beds so that in the very early spring, color is evident in all parts of the garden. An added benefit is that these bulbs were deep planted; once the leaves have finished their work and are pruned off, the soil can be cultivated without fear of hitting a bulb. The perennial foliage then overgrows the area, preventing excessive weed growth. Single early tulips have good upright flower stems that resist spring weather damage.

Double Early Tulips

Height: 12–18 inches

Flower Size: 3 inches

Bloom Time: First to second week of May in zone 4

Planting Depth: 3 inches

Spacing: 2–4 inches

Planting Time: Fall, best after September

Sunlight Needed: Full sun

Tulipa 'Electra' (double early)

Double early tulips resemble the single early tulips in growth habit; but the doubles produce many irregularly shaped petals to form a flower that resembles a stubby peony bloom. Although I am not enamored of double blossoms, preferring instead the singles, these early doubles do come in a full range of colors: whites through yellow to red, including some with striped edges and flecked blooms. Many gardeners enjoy these fully double flowers, and breeders are working to introduce new cultivars. The double blooms last as well as the single blooms, and there is no difference in their cultivation requirements. The only problem that they exhibit is that many larger double-flowering plants are susceptible to bowing over when filled with the weight of rainwater or when pushed around by spring storms.

Triumph Tulips

Height: 8–24 inches
Bloom Time: Second to third week of May in zone 4
Depth to Plant: 3–8 inches
Spacing: 2–4 inches
Best Season to Plant: Fall
Sunlight Needed: Full sun

Tulipa 'Attila' (triumph)

Breeding the single early tulips with the single late tulips produced the triumph tulip, which blooms in midseason. There is an extremely wide range of colors in this class, from the reddish purple tones of 'Attila', to the orange-yellow and red of 'Fidelio', the ivory white of 'White Dream', and the yellow with red flames of 'Washington'. The stems on this class are of medium length, so they stand up with some authority to late spring storms. The strength of the stem also means that they make excellent forcing tulips.

Darwin Hybrid Tulips

Height: 14–20 inches

Bloom Time: Second to third week of May in zone 4

Depth to Plant: 3–8 inches

Spacing: 2–4 inches

Best Season to Plant: Fall

Sunlight Needed: Full sun

Tulipa 'Apeldoorn' (Darwin hybrid)

The Darwin hybrids make up an interesting class of flowers; the breeders crossed *T. Fosteriana* 'Madame Lefeber' and cultivars of the original Darwin tulips (now in the single late class) to obtain a class of hybrids with the largest flowers of any tulip. Because of the huge flowers and strong stems, they are a favorite for the forcing trade; if you purchase cut tulips in the winter, they will be Darwin hybrids. These same huge flowers and strong stems make them a favorite for large municipal plantings, where they deliver quite a bit of color. Although they are limited in colors to tones of red, orange, pink, and yellow, they are among the most well-liked tulips. Popular varieties include 'Apeldoorn', a brilliant vermilion red; 'Elizabeth Arden', a salmon pink; 'Orange Sun', a deep orange; and 'President Kennedy', a gold yellow with red-lined edges.

Single Late Tulips

Height: 16–30 inches

Bloom Time: Fourth week of May to first week of June in zone 4

Depth to Plant: 3–8 inches

Spacing: 2–4 inches

Best Season to Plant: Fall

Sunlight Needed: Full sun

Tulipa 'Douglas Baader' (single late)

The single late class is a new class that combines tulips previously known as breeder, Darwin, and cottage tulips. All the varieties bloom late in the season and have fairly long and strong stems. These are the tallest of the tulips, generally towering over the earlier classes. There is a full range of colors, from the light scarlet of 'Advance', to the clear white of 'Alabaster', to the soft, pale pink of 'Douglas Baader'. 'Queen of Night' is a black maroon, one of the darkest tulips, which gives an interesting effect when mass planted. This is a popular variety that some catalogs list as 'Queen of *the* Night'. It is the same plant, just a small mistake in the proper name.

Lily-Flowered Tulips

Height: 16–24 inches
Bloom Time: Fourth week of May to first week of
   June in zone 4
Depth to Plant: 3–8 inches
Spacing: 2–4 inches
Best Season to Plant: Fall
Sunlight Needed: Full sun

Tulipa 'Aladdin' (lily-flowered)

There are not as many varieties of lily-flowering tulips as there are in other classes, but they more than make up for their small numbers with their colors and flower form. The flowers have pointed petals that curve backward as they reach the top of the blossom and are quite distinctive. The color range is quite good and includes some very powerful and shimmering shades. 'China Pink' is a luminous carmine pink, 'Ballade' is a bright violet with white edges, 'Aladdin' is a deep red with yellow edges, and the more sedate 'Marilyn' is white flushed with pink. To really set a striking tone in the garden, plant clumps of 'Red Shine', a bright red; 'West Point', a bright yellow; and 'White Triumphator', a pure clear white. The stems of this class are fairly strong, and the flowers are not so large as to create a wind-tossed look in the garden. Plant them with confidence.

Fringed Tulips

Height: 10–30 inches

Bloom Time: Fourth week of May to first week of June in zone 4

Depth to Plant: 3–8 inches

Spacing: 2–4 inches

Best Season to Plant: Fall

Sunlight Needed: Full sun

Tulipa 'Fancy Frills' (fringed)

Fringed tulips look as if someone took a pair of scissors to the petals and finely fringed them. Quite elegant looking, easy to grow, and reasonably weather resistant, they are becoming ever more popular. The lacy-looking petals come in a variety of sizes and colors, ranging from the tall 'Maja' at 26 inches with a pale yellow crystalline fringe to 'Fancy Frills' at 16 inches with an ivory white blending with rose pink. These tulips should be displayed in prime garden locations, because their delicate petals may be lost in the crowd of spring blooms. The blossoms survive normal spring winds and rains, but very heavy downpours or winds will damage them.

Viridiflora Tulips

Height: 18–24 inches

Bloom Time: Third week of May to first week of June in zone 4

Depth to Plant: 3–8 inches

Spacing: 2–4 inches

Best Season to Plant: Fall

Sunlight Needed: Full sun

Tulipa 'Red Pimpernel' (viridiflora)

If you know your Latin, you will know that the class name *viridiflora* can be broken down into *viridi,* meaning "green," and *flora,* meaning "flower." This class of tulips has green-striped flowers; and although they are not common in the garden world, they are found in some catalogs. Easily grown, they are a conversation point in many gardens. One characteristic that endears them to the heart of those that like them is their very long flowering time, much longer than the other classes of tulips. The green in modern varieties is usually a medium-width green stripe that runs from the base to the tip of the petal. Varieties include 'Golden Artist', golden yellow and green; 'Red Pimpernel', a purplish red and green; 'Greenland', soft pink and green; and 'Spring Green', soft white and green. These make excellent cut flowers.

Rembrandt Tulips

Height: 16–30 inches

Bloom Time: Fourth week of May to first week of June in zone 4

Depth to Plant: 3–8 inches

Spacing: 2–4 inches

Best Season to Plant: Fall

Sunlight Needed: Full sun

Tulipa 'Malak' (Rembrandt)

The original Rembrandt tulips are no longer available for sale and are not actively cultivated. The original bulbs were from the Darwin class and produced mottled, streaked, and two-toned petals. In fact, these colors were not the result of breeding but were instead the result of viral infections. Although they were immensely popular in their day, the colors were not stable, and the virus could infect other tulips. Instead of the original Rembrandts, today we have several look-alike bulbs that are genetically stable and whose colors are the result of breeding, not disease. Most mail-order companies carry a mixed lot of these tulips, and named varieties are not always available.

Parrot Tulips

Height: 16–20 inches

Bloom Time: Third to fourth week of May in zone 4

Depth to Plant: 3–8 inches

Spacing: 2–4 inches

Best Season to Plant: Fall

Sunlight Needed: Full sun

Tulipa 'Texas Flame' (Parrot)

Once you see parrot tulips, you will never forget them. Each petal is heavily fringed; there is no mistaking them for any other class of tulip. A second characteristic that may confuse new gardeners is their tendency to stay green or have large green spots on the petals right up to the time they open. These green spots will disappear, but the buds look "unripe" for the longest time.

Parrot tulips have large flowers and very supple stems. This means that early summer storms can punish them terribly; so plant them only in protected areas of the garden. Although the flowers mostly open horizontally, the color spectrum is good, ranging from the violet black of 'Black Parrot', to the mauve of 'Blue Parrot', and the brilliant red of 'Erna Lindgreen'. The pinks are represented by 'Fantasy', a bright pink; and the yellows include 'Texas Gold', a bright yellow, and 'Texas Flame', a yellow-and-red combination.

Double Late Tulips; Peony-Flowered Tulips

Height: 12–16 inches

Bloom Time: Fourth week of May to first week of June in zone 4

Depth to Plant: 3–8 inches

Spacing: 2–4 inches

Best Season to Plant: Fall

Sunlight Needed: Full sun

Tulipa 'Allegretto' (double late)

The double late tulip class produces a flower that looks more like a peony than a tulip. These large flowers are extremely weather sensitive and suffer in rain or wind. So plant them in a very protected area of the garden; and if a storm threatens, cut the open blooms for the kitchen table. The color range of the doubles tends to the red spectrum; the most popular cultivars include 'Allegretto', a yellow-edged red; 'Derbrand Kieft', a white-edged red; 'Kastrup', a two-toned red; and 'May Wonder', a bright pink.

Kaufmanniana Tulips
Height: 4–8 inches
Bloom Time: First week of May in zone 4
Depth to Plant: 3 inches
Spacing: 2–4 inches
Best Season to Plant: Fall
Sunlight Needed: Full sun

Tulipa 'Ancilla' (Kaufmanniana)

Kaufmanniana tulips are short plants that open their petals in full sunlight and close down in dull weather. The inside of the flower petals is usually a brighter shade than the outside; this creates a shimmering or wonderfully bold contrasting look, depending on the amount of color contrast. Being short, these plants do best in the rock garden or at the front of borders where they can be fully appreciated. Plant them in large numbers so the full effect of their coloration can be seen and enjoyed. These bulbs do multiply if happy, so quite a colony will form. Good cultivars include 'Johann Strauss', a medium red with pale yellow edging; 'Ancilla', a bright deep pink with medium green foliage; and 'Showwinner', a good cardinal red with spotted foliage.

Fosteriana Tulips

Height: 12–18 inches
Bloom Time: First to second week of May in zone 4
Depth to Plant: 3–8 inches
Spacing: 2–4 inches
Best Season to Plant: Fall
Sunlight Needed: Full sun

Tulipa 'Red Emperor' (Fosteriana)

Fosteriana tulips bloom with the daffodils and can make a spectacular combination if complementary colors are chosen. Native to the mountains of central Asia, they are hardy and have good weather resistance. They are excellent for naturalizing and make wonderful cut flowers. Plant them and forget them—except in the spring, when they will remind you of their presence. Some good cultivars include 'Easter Moon', yellow with yellow-edged leaves, and 'Yellow Empress', an oblong-shaped tulip, well worth the effort to find. 'Red Emperor' (sometimes sold as 'Madame Lefeber') is a solid fire-engine red with a black interior encircled in yellow; it is a spectacular old standby.

Greigii Tulips

Height: 8–12 inches
Bloom Time: First to third week of May in zone 4
Depth to Plant: 3 inches
Spacing: 2–4 inches
Best Season to Plant: Fall
Sunlight Needed: Full sun

Tulipa 'Red Riding Hood' (Greigii)

Greigii tulips, native to Turkistan, are known for their bright colors and wonderful foliage. Easily grown, these shorter-flowering bulbs are perfect for the front of the border, in the rock garden, or mixed with shorter daffodils in naturalized settings. The stems on these bulbs are quite rigid, giving them an excellent weather tolerance and holding the flowers so they can open up to the sun. Popular varieties include 'Red Riding Hood', a shining vermilion red with spotted foliage; 'Corsage', a soft coral orange with yellow edging and spotted foliage; 'Oratorio', a watermelon pink with spotted foliage; and 'Plaisir', a carmine red with white edges and spotted foliage. Most of the Greigii tulips have a darker heart, or center, of the interior flower, giving them a two-toned look. Note that sometimes bulb dealers offer Greigii tulips mixes under the name peacock tulips.

Multiflowered Tulips

Height: 10 inches
Bloom Time: First to second week of May in zone 4
Depth to Plant: 3–8 inches
Spacing: 2–4 inches
Best Season to Plant: Fall
Sunlight Needed: Full sun

Tulipa 'Georgette' (multiflowered)

The multiflowered group is not actually a "class" of tulip but a grouping of plants that share a single characteristic: each stem breaks into secondary stems so that a single bulb can produce between 3 and 7 flowers. Commonly available varieties include 'Toronto', salmon pink with purple-mottled foliage; 'Georgette', yellow with red spots; and 'Red Georgette', deep red with a black-and-yellow interior. They are reasonably weather resistant and as easy to grow as the other tulip classes. The flowers on the main stem tend to be the same size as the single late class, whereas the side shoots produce smaller flowers.

A SELECTION OF SPECIES TULIPS

Name	Height	Color	Comments
Tulipa acuminata	16 inches	Yellow; red marbled	Petals long and narrow, ending in fringed points
Tulipa bakeri	6 inches	Pinkish; orange-yellow heart; white edging	Cheerful
Tulipa batalinii	6 inches	Gold yellow	Petals pointed; star-shaped flower
Tulipa chrysantha	6 inches	Yellow or red	Blue-and-green foliage; hardy; easy and attractive
Tulipa clusiana	12 inches	Reds to pinks; vertical stripes	Star-shaped flower; wonderful
Tulipa eichleri	10 inches	Red- and yellow-striped; black spot in interior	Big flowers with pointed petals; likes to spread
Tulip kolpakowskiana	8 inches	Yellow; red flush	Small star-shaped flower; sometimes two blooms on a stem
Tulipa linifolia	4 inches	Unique fluorescent red	Pointed petals open in sun; curve backward to form cup shape
Tulipa marjolettii	20 inches	Yellow-and-red flamed	Pointed petals; gray-green foliage narrow and quite long
Tulipa pulchella	6 inches	Purple-violet with darker base	Crocus-shaped flowers; foliage often red-edged; plant in sheltered space
Tulipa saxatilis	12 inches	Mauve pink	Large star-shaped flower; likes rocky soils
Tulipa tarda	4 inches	Gold yellow with white point	Star-shaped flower; multiplies rapidly.
Tulipa turkestanica	8 inches	White and cream; darker heart	Similar to *T. tarda*, except taller and petals more pointed
Tulipa urumiensis	2 inches	Bright yellow	Opens to sun, closes to clouds; short lived; needs summer drying to survive

Species Tulips

Species tulips, each with its own particular mountainous habitat, are lumped into this class. Use these bulbs in rock gardens, the very front of borders in conspicuous locations, or in naturalized settings. When planted in small clumps, as they are found in nature, they bring a wonderful wild charm to the spring garden. As a class, they like their summers dry and hot. If happy, they will multiply; and some, like *T. tarda,* can become a nuisance. Cultivate out

Tulipa bakeri (species)

any unwanted bulbs, and share them with friends. The flowering period of the species bulbs is invariably early in the season. The bulbs listed in "A Selection of Species Tulips" are those found most often in catalogs.

Tulipa saxatilis (species)

Tulipa bakeri (species)

easy summer bloomers

The Essentials

- Plant Portraits for Easy Summer Bloomers

Once the spring-flowering bulbs have given us a much-needed boost after a winter of blossom deprivation, the flamboyant darlings of summer take over. Some of these bulbs are best treated as annuals in the colder areas of the continent, but all are wonderful bloomers worthy of garden space.

Plant Portraits for Easy Summer Bloomers

Anemone coronaria

Poppy-flowered anemone
Height: 12 inches
Bloom time: June to July in zone 4
Depth to Plant: 4 inches
Spacing: 8–12 inches
Best Season to Plant: Varies by location
Sunlight Needed: Full sun to light shade

Anemone coronaria

Like many of the bulbs, the anemone was named after a fallen classical hero. In this case, the likely culprit is Adonis, beloved of Aphrodite (we got to *anemone* through a corrupted Greek translation of the Semitic word for Adonis, *Naaman*). A wild bore gored this poor god of flowers to death. He disappeared into the ground in the fall and winter, and apparently reappeared each spring along with the bloodred blooms of the anemone. There are two species of anemone commonly found in bulb catalogs: *A. blanda* and *A. coronaria*. *A. blanda* varieties are described in Part Three (page 51).

A. coronaria is a summer sweetheart and is described here. This bulb is hardy in zones 7–10, where it is planted in the fall. Outside of these areas, and especially in northern gardens, it is treated as an annual bulb. In the spring, plant anemone bulbs after there is no danger of frost and when the ground is warming up. Two tips that I learned from an older gardener are to always soak these bulbs in tepid water for a few hours before planting and to plant them on their edges. Both tips work for me when I plant anemone.

Plant these poppy-flowered anemones in the spring and enjoy the blooms. When the foliage starts to fade, dig up the bulbs and keep them in a cool, dry place until the following spring. Store them in dry peat or sand; and do not water them at all, because they require a dry dormancy to set their flowers for the following year. Although a serious anemone gardener would be shocked, it must be pointed out that, because they are so inexpensive, the 'DeCaen' and 'St. Bridgit' anemones are often treated as annuals and left to die after flowering.

There are two strains of *A. coronaria* commonly available in catalogs. The 'DeCaen' cultivars have poppylike blooms, such as 'Hollandia', with its bright scarlet petals. The second strain is the 'St. Bridgit' cultivars with double flowers in a variety of scarlets, blues, roses, and white. Treat both types in the same manner. Although *A. blanda* will tolerate summer wet, *A. coronaria* will quickly go downhill if kept damp for the summer.

Dahlia

Dahlia

Height: 1–8 feet

Bloom time: Third week of June to frost in zone 4

Depth to Plant: 1–2 inches for small forms; 4 inches for large forms

Spacing: 6–8 inches for small forms, 18 inches for large forms

Best Season to Plant: Spring, after frost

Sunlight Needed: Full sun

Dahlia mix

To grow a great standard dahlia (not the smaller ones grown as bedding plants), there are a few important tips to follow. The first and most important of these is to under-

Different dahlia flower forms: (1) single, (2) anemone, (3) Colarette, (4) ball, (5) pompon, (6) decorative, (7) decorative fimbriated, (8) water lily, (9) cactus, (10) semicactus, (11) peony, (12) star, (13) orchid

stand that the dahlia is one of the greediest feeders in the garden. This plant will do really well only if several shovelsful of compost are worked into the soil before planting, and it demands a liquid feeding several times a month throughout the growing season. The only plants that share this need for nutrition in my garden are roses, corn, and tomatoes. A second tip is to watch for aphids on the growing shoots. These tiny plant lice will stunt the growth of the young shoots, ruining the blossoms if unchecked.

If a truly wonderful dahlia is desired, allow the plant to grow unchecked until it reaches approximately 12 inches tall; then pinch off the growing tips. Pinching off these growing tips will force the plant to create additional shoots, each of which will bear flowers. If you'd like, carry this an additional step forward: When the flower buds form, there will be a primary central bud and immediately below that two or more ancillary buds. If you pick off the ancillary buds, allowing only the central bud to develop, the remaining flower will be truly spectacular.

Taller dahlias benefit from staking. This is a gardener's way of saying that staking is really necessary to keep the taller dahlias upright against the wind and rain. Put the stakes into the ground when the tubers are planted; the top of the stake should be 12 inches below the mature height of the dahlia plant. Use a soft twine or old stocking to hold the growing stem to the stake, making sure you haven't tied it too tight or cut into the soft stem. The stake must be quite firmly planted, as tall dahlias will develop a significant flower head weight. Stakes do look out of place in an elegant garden, which is one reason dahlias are often given a place of their own in larger gardens. If you are growing dahlias for their cut flowers, place them in the vegetable garden. With sundry stakes and cages, the dahlias will fit right in.

When the first frost just blackens the tips of the dahlias, dig them up, knock the excess soil from the roots, and allow them to dry in a frost-free area. A tip I learned from reading an old gardening magazine from the 1800s was to thrust a sharp spike (or long screwdriver) down through the old stem, right through the tuber. This allows any excess moisture to evaporate and not collect to rot the tuber. I have stored tubers both ways, with and without piercing; and as long as the tuber is kept dry and cool, there does not appear to be any benefit to piercing. Many helpful gardening friends will still let you in on the piercing secret; it cannot hurt, and it might even help. After the soil is well dried on the tubers, knock off as much of it as possible and store the dahlias in a cool, dark, dry location until the following spring when it's time to replant.

After a few years, the dahlia tuber will become large enough to divide. Although this division sometimes happens by accident as the tuber is being dug from the garden, the usual method is to divide them in the spring just before planting. Division is easy. Cut the tuber apart using a sharp knife, ensuring that each section has a tiny eye. The eye is usually a pinkish point on the tuber and is normally close to the center of the plant and the old stem rather than on the outer edge of the tuber. All sections with an eye will produce flowers in their first year of planting.

Sections without an eye do not normally grow. Often, small sections will be knocked off the main tuber during fall or spring handling. If these have an eye, store or plant them; discard if there is no eye.

Galtonia candicans

Summer Hyacinth

Height: 24–30 inches

Bloom time: First week of August in zone 4

Depth to Plant: 2–4

Spacing: 4 inches

Best Season to Plant: Fall

Sunlight Needed: Full sun to light shade

Galtonia is often described in English bulb books as being quite tender. They survive nicely in my not-so-tender garden for several reasons. The most important is that they are placed in a soil that has excellent drainage. The lack of standing water in the summer and winter (when the ground is frozen) may contribute to

Galtonia candicans

their survival; in more temperate regions, surface freezing and thawing can cause the soil to become waterlogged, which will harm galtonia bulbs. Plant this bulb in a location where it will not receive any winter moisture. Their wonderful white spires in early August regularly come as a pleasant surprise in my late-summer garden. The blooms last several weeks, and although many books claim this bulb is quite fragrant, my specimens have only the mildest of perfumes. Of the three galtonia species, *G. candicans* is the bulb commonly found in catalogs; and it comes highly recommended. The other two bulbs are not commonly available outside collector circles and, being African, are suited only for the warmest of gardens. Once established, try not to move them, because galtonia resent being disturbed.

Gladiolus

Sword Lily
Height: 36–48 inches
Bloom time: July to August in zone 4
Depth to Plant: 4–6 inches
Spacing: 6–8 inches
Best Season to Plant: Spring, after frost
Sunlight Needed: Full sun for best results

Gladiolus

There are approximately 180 species of gladiolus found in the wild, but our garden glads are thought to be the result of hybridization of seven African species. The genus name *Gladiolus* is Latin for "sword," obviously referring to the swordlike leaves of the plant. Glads like a sunny spot in the garden and fertile, well-drained soil. Working compost into the soil before planting is an excellent way to keep them happy and growing.

I used to grow glads commercially, and I will pass along several tips learned from years of growing thousands of these beauties in my back fields. The first is that some authors will routinely tell you to plant them carefully; bottom side down. As described in "Bulb-Planting Techniques" on page 10, I used to plant these bulbs with a tractor and plow; however they landed at the bottom of the trench was fine with me and the bulb. Most early varieties will flower 80 days from the day they are planted; later, larger bloomers will flower 100 days after planting. Stagger plantings 7 to 10 days apart to achieve a continuous succession of blooms. I started planting the corms as soon as the ground was warm enough to plant sweet-corn seed (usually the second week of May in zone 4) and would plant every week after that until the second week of June. Sometimes the last plantings would get hit by a fall frost; but if the budded stalks were picked before the frost, they would open up quite nicely anyway. Avoid crooked stems by watering regularly and applying a low-nitrogen, high-potash liquid fertilizer around the growing stems every 10 days. That is a short lesson in the commercial growing of gladiolus bulbs, but the techniques are the same for the home garden.

Winter storage is as simple as digging up the bulbs just after the first frost and allowing them to thoroughly dry out in a warm sunny spot. Once well dried, knock off the remaining soil chunks, remove the stem, and clean the bulb well. Store in a cool, dry, dark area with lots of ventilation for the winter. Check the bulbs regularly; and if any rotting is evident, throw out the victims. Good sanitation is quite important when storing glads; and the cleaner the bulb is going into the storage area, the better its chances of survival.

Iris (Later-Flowering)

Later-Flowering Iris

The spring-flowering bulbous or tuberous iris are discussed in Part Three (page 65); here the later-flowering rhizomatous and fibrous-rooted types of iris are described. There are more than 200 species of iris in the wild; selecting just a few to grow can be quite a challenge once you're smitten by the beauty of the flowers and the relative ease of growing this class. I say *relative ease* because some types of iris are adapted to the warmer parts of the continent and others to the colder parts; trying to grow iris out of its natural habitat will definitely lead to frustration. I will outline the more easily available iris and discuss their cultural needs.

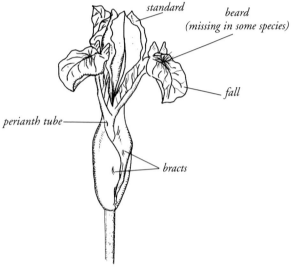

Parts of an iris flower.

standard

beard
(missing in some species)

fall

perianth tube

bracts

Bearded Iris

Height: 6–36 inches (see page 110)
Bloom time: Second to fourth week of June in zone 4
Depth to Plant: On soil surface
Spacing: 12 inches for dwarfs; 24 inches for tall
Best Season to Plant: Early fall
Sunlight Needed: Full sun (see text for exceptions)

Bearded iris make up the single most popular class of iris grown in gardens today; there are literally thousands of registered varieties. The bearded class comes in a full range of heights and colors so they can be grown in almost any kind of garden, if their primary needs are met. To flower well, bearded iris require a well-drained soil in full sunshine. They need a sandy

Iris 'Grand Waltz' (bearded)

soil and, unlike many plants, do not greatly benefit from large applications of compost. A small handful in the spring will help with the flower size. If the bearded iris is planted in clay soils, the excess water will lead to rotting of the rhizome. On the other hand, if the drainage is good, the bearded iris is one of the hardest garden plants to kill.

The bearded iris does have one peculiar habit that all gardeners should be aware of: If the rhizome is buried when planting, the leaves will be large and lush, but the flowers will be nonexistent. To obtain good flowers, plant the rhizome so that it remains on the surface, but the roots should be well anchored into the soil. Planting is as simple as digging a trench and laying the roots against one of its walls. Backfill the trench, making sure the roots are well covered and the rhizome is not. In gardens in the South, where heat is a problem, it may be advisable to cover the rhizome slightly, ever so slightly, to prevent it from being scorched. If you apply fertilizer, use a low-nitrogen, high-potash form.

Choose bearded iris cultivars based on the height required for your garden and the appropriate flower color. Catalogs will use the abbreviations listed in "Bearded Iris Heights," below, when describing heights. In general, irises of a similar height will flower at the same time; the shortest varieties flower a couple of weeks before the tallest. In this way, you can obtain a longer period of iris bloom or can pick the blooms to fit a particular color combination.

BEARDED IRIS HEIGHTS

Name	Abbreviation	Height
Miniature dwarf bearded	MDB	< 8 inches
Standard dwarf bearded	SDB	8–16 inches
Intermediate bearded	IB	16–27 inches
Miniature tall bearded	MTB	16–27 inches
Border bearded	BB	16–27 inches
Tall bearded	TB	> 27 inches

Another practical note to be aware of when choosing iris varieties is that catalogs will identify some iris as "remontant." These plants flower twice in one season: once in the early summer and again in the fall. To ensure remontant iris have the strength to continue to bloom, it is useful to feed them after their first bloom with a handful of low-nitrogen, high-potash fertilizer.

The tall bearded class requires staking in my garden. I am not sure why this happens, but just about when the flowers are starting to look their best in my garden, a storm comes up and knocks these top-heavy plants to the ground. I can count on it. Use a short stake and tie the stems with a soft cord or something that does not show against the leaves. One alternative is to pray for sunshine for the 2 weeks the iris are in bloom. My choice was to stop growing the taller bearded varieties and concentrate on the shorter forms.

Beardless Iris

Height: 3 feet
Bloom time: Second to fourth week of June in zone 4
Depth to Plant: Roots into the ground
Spacing: 24 inches
Best Season to Plant: Early fall
Sunlight Needed: Full sun or part shade

Iris sibirica 'Ruffled Velvet' (beardless)

Although beardless iris obviously differ from the bearded types by the absence of a beard on the flower, they also differ for the most part in the way they can be grown. The most commonly found iris in this group is the Siberian iris, which comes in hundreds of wonderful hybrids. Siberian iris are plants of meadows and sunny woodland areas in their native habitat, and that tells us we can grow them in the sunny perennial border or in a part-shade environment. Because they naturally exist in woodland areas means they like a humus-rich soil and adequate moisture with good drainage; if you provide these two things, a wonderful flower show will result. These are slow-spreading, clump-forming plants with extensive root systems, unlike the bearded class, which have rhizomes. Some nurseries sell Siberian iris as water-side plants, and although this is not a preferred habitat, they will survive (but not thrive) in damp soils. If your garden areas are wet, don't despair; some iris thrive in damp soils.

Plant beardless iris as you would any other rooted plant; put the roots into the ground, cover, and water thoroughly. There is no need to worry about the depth of the planting roots, although deeply burying the leaves is not advised. Not only is the plant hardy in most colder gardening zones, but it is weather resistant. While the bearded iris are flopping on the ground after a heavy rain, the Siberian iris, with its stiff upright stems and smaller flowers, are almost rainproof and continue to provide a show during downpours.

Pacific Coast Iris
Height: 3 feet
Bloom time: Second to fourth week of June in zone 7
Depth to Plant: Roots into the ground
Spacing: 24 inches
Best Season to Plant: Early fall
Sunlight Needed: Part shade

The Pacific coast iris comprise 11 species, and they have some specific needs. They grow best in neutral to acid soils in slight shade. If grown in alkaline soils, they will lose vigor, slowly decline, and die. A warm-weather lover, Pacific coast iris are frost sensitive and so are seldom seen (alive, in any case) in areas north of zones 6–7. They are available from mail-order houses that specialize in iris.

Laevigata Iris
The laevigata iris love wet spaces and are found in ditches and swamps throughout North America, Asia, and Europe.

I. pseudacorus, I. versicolor
Height: 3–4 feet
Bloom time: Second to fourth week of June in zone 4
Depth to Plant: Roots into the ground
Spacing: 24 inches
Best Season to Plant: Early fall
Sunlight Needed: Full sun

Yellow flag iris (*I. pseudacorus*) is a well-known North American native as is the blue flag (*I. versicolor*) of eastern North American. These two iris are easily grown beside a pond or as a shallow-water plant if the soil line is at or slightly below the water line. Yellow and blue flags are hardy and easy to grow; when they get too large, simply chop them apart, move them about, and replant the small pieces. Often found in garden centers or catalogs, these are wonderfully easy plants for the iris novice. Plant them as you would a bearded iris.

I. ensata
Height: 3–4 feet, depending on cultivar
Bloom time: Third week of June to second week July in zone 4
Depth to Plant: Roots into the ground
Spacing: 24 inches
Best Season to Plant: Early fall
Sunlight Needed: Full sun

Japanese iris (*I. ensata*; a synonym is *I. kaempferi*) is also a wonderful water-side plant. Success with it depends on a constant supply of moisture, an acid soil high in humus, and a dryer spot for winter storage. This is generally not a plant for beginners, but it is often found in catalogs. Most people have success when they grow Japanese iris as a potted plant sunk in the ground beside a pond. Use a 50:50 mix of potting soil and peat moss in the pot, and then dig up the entire pot and store inside in a cool spot for the winter.

Louisiana Iris

Height: 2–4 feet, depending on the cultivar

Bloom time: First week of July in zone 7

Depth to Plant: Roots into the ground

Spacing: 24 inches

Best Season to Plant: Early fall

Sunlight Needed: Full sun

Louisiana iris are water-loving plants, found in the swamps of the southern United States. They are quite easy to grow if you have a long, hot season and damp soil but are impossible in the northern areas where the days and growing season are both short. Southern gardeners with a good damp spot in the garden should search out some of the newer cultivars in iris catalogs. Do not waste your time if your garden does not meet the cultural requirements.

Leucojum autumnale

Snowflake

Height: 6 inches

Bloom time: Third to fourth week of August in zone 4

Depth to Plant: 3–4 inches

Spacing: 2–3 inches

Best Season to Plant: Fall

Sunlight Needed: Full sun

Leucojum autumnale

This snowflake differs from its spring-blooming cousins in several ways. The first and most obvious is that it blooms much later in the season than the spring bloomers described on page 70. Second, it does not like damp areas, preferring instead the sunnier, dryer parts of the garden. Slightly tender and unreliable in zone 4, it much prefers the longer season of zone 5 gardens. The white, bell-like flowers superficially resemble *Galanthus* (page 61), which, along with *L. autumnale,* are called snowdrops in some parts of the country. *L. autumnale* is well worth hunting down for its perennial charm.

Lilium

Lily

When the lilies bloom, everything else in the garden pales in comparison. Visitors do not ask about the rare perennials blooming beside them; they want to know only about the lilies. If I were a poet, this is where I would be waxing poetic about the lily's gorgeous blooms. Unfortunately, poetry genes were left out of my makeup, so I can only tell you to grow some of these beauties to give your summer garden a lift.

Lilium (Asiatic and Oriental mix)

Replicating the lily's natural habitat in the garden will ensure the bulb grows to its potential; luckily, this is relatively easy for most gardeners. The majority of lilies like slightly acid soils, so dig some peat moss into the lily bed. Peat not only acidifies the soil but will eventually add to the high humus content that lilies demand if they are to perform well. To further increase the humus level, add several shovelsful of compost per square foot of garden area, digging it in at least as deep as the shovel blade before planting. Topdress every spring with compost.

Most lilies have contractile roots so they will adjust their depth downward (but not upward) to suit themselves. Initial plantings should be 3–4 inches deep. A rule of thumb is to multiply the depth of the bulb in inches by two, and then plant so the top of the bulb is that deep in the ground. For example, suppose the bulb's depth is 2 inches. Then $2 \times 2 = 4$ inches. Thus the top of the bulb should be 4 inches below the surface of the soil. This deep planting helps stabilize the bulb against the weight of the flower stalk. The only exception to this rule is the Madonna lily (*L. candidum*), which should be planted just below the surface. An important growing point that many

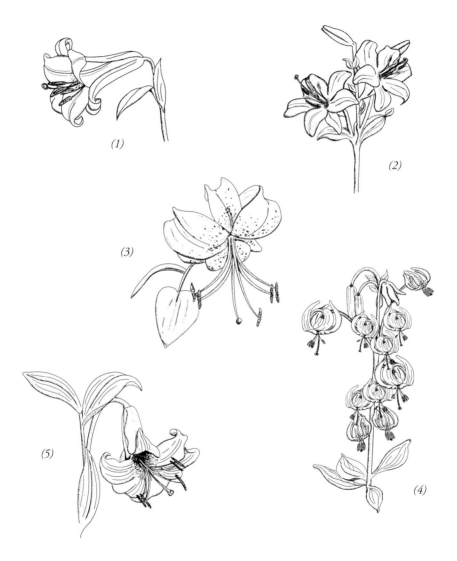

Lily classes: (1) trumpet and Aurelian, (2) Madonna, (3) Oriental, (4) martagon or Turk's-cap, (5)Asiatic

gardeners forget is that better lilies result when the bulbs are shaded but the leaves grow up into the sunshine. Planting them out in the full hot, baking sun is a sure recipe for eventual disappointment. If your garden is in full sun, then cover the bulb bed with 3–4 inches of your favorite mulch, which will serve the same purpose. A good planting design is to mix the bulbs into the general perennial border or between evergreens and shrubs. The other plants will help stabilize and hold the lily stems up during bad weather and will provide the needed shade for the bulbs.

Given that there are approximately 4,600 species of plants in the lily family, it is simply not possible to describe every one. I should tell you that I've never met one I did not like; but to make things easy, this section includes descriptions of lily bulbs normally available in catalogs. To choose a lily for your garden, first pick the flower form; then look through catalogs or garden center shelves for a color and height that matches your garden design. The growing conditions for all lilies are as described above.

Be sure to plant large clumps of the same type of lily. Mass planting is much more effective than spreading the bulbs singly around the garden. Also note that it is better to have fewer kinds of lilies in the garden and more bulbs of each kind than to have one bulb each of many different kinds. The magazine garden pictures that we all love to dream about never consist of a single bloom. Mass planting brings the dream to reality.

Trumpet and Aurelian Lilies

Height: 4–6 feet
Bloom time: Third week of June to third week July in zone 4
Depth to Plant: 4 to 6 inches
Spacing: 6–8 inches
Best Season to Plant: Early fall
Sunlight Needed: Leaves in full sun; bulb shaded

The trumpet-shaped blooms of these lilies are the classic flower form that we all imagine a lily to be. These are the tallest of the garden lilies, easily reaching 4–6 feet, towering over the garden. With their outward-facing, horizontal flowers on strong stalks, they put on quite a show. These lilies appreciate some stem support, either from staking or surrounding perennials, because the plant's height and huge flower size are its own worst enemies in windstorms. A July flowering time in my garden gives them place of pride, and there are few worthy competitors for attention when they start to flower. The fragrance is evident in some cultivars but is not overpowering. Note that the regal lily (*L. regale*), from China, is one of the parents of this group and is itself worthy of growing in the garden.

L. candidum

Height: 3 feet
Bloom time: Second to third week of July in zone 4
Depth to Plant: 1 inch
Spacing: 6–8 inches
Best Season to Plant: Early fall
Sunlight Needed: Leaves in full sun; bulb shaded

The Madonna lily is the only single lily discussed here because it is one of the oldest plants in cultivation and because it is quite unusual in its habits. Let me say at the outset that I have a small patch of this lily in one of the places of honor in my garden; I pass it every day walking to the nursery and delight in it when it blooms. Plant this lily so it is only 1 inch below the surface; it thrives on this shallow planting. The Madonna lily is the only bulb that will throw a rosette of leaves in the fall. This rosette stays all winter, waiting for spring, and is quite natural. Do not weed out the rosette thinking it is an unwanted plant taking over the bulb patch. (This has been done more than once by beginners.)

Do plant your Madonna lilies away from all other lilies. Garden folklore is very clear that they are more likely to succumb to fungus and viral problems when planted among other lilies then when planted alone. Plus, they do not like competition. Their natural beauty should stand apart in any case. The clear white flowers on 3–4-foot-high sturdy stems are held horizontally and are quite visible down into the base of the flower. The bright yellow of the pollen emphasizes the yellow interior tones. The fragrance is quite delicate but unmistakable. This is a very desirable bulb for the garden.

Oriental Lilies

Height: 3 feet

Bloom time: Third week of June to third week of July in zone 4

Depth to Plant: 4–6 inches

Spacing: 8–12 inches

Best Season to Plant: Early fall

Sunlight Needed: Leaves in full sun; bulb shaded

The Oriental class of hybrid lilies was developed by crossing the Korean lily (*L. speciosum*) with the Japanese forms (*L. auratum, L. japonicum,* and *L. rubellum*), which are all wonderfully beautiful lilies in themselves. Oriental lilies are hardy to zone 4; and if a powerful fragrance and huge flower display are desired, this class cannot be ignored. Oriental bulbs tend to be more expensive than other classes, but one whiff of their perfumed blossoms and any thought of saving money will vanish. The parent lilies are known to be susceptible to fungal diseases, and this characteristic is variable in the hybrids. Do give them a bit of extra room to ensure good air circulation; note that the recommended spacing is 8–12 inches instead of the more usual 6–8 inches. The size of the blossoms will demand this extra space.

Most of the flowers are held horizontally or slightly upright for good viewing, although a few hybrids have a pendulous habit (downward facing). Look at the pictures or read the descriptions carefully in the catalogs to be sure you buy the flower form you want. For example, one of the strongest and best—and thus most readily available—varieties is 'Sans Souci'; it has a semipendulous habit, which means it tends to face downward. Plant these lilies in large clumps, and the downward-facing habit will not be a problem when they bloom on their 4-foot-tall stems.

L. Martagon

Height: 3–5 feet

Bloom time: Second to third week of July zone 4

Depth to Plant: 4 to 6 inches

Spacing: 6–9 inches

Best Season to Plant: Early fall

Sunlight Needed: Leaves in full sun; bulb shaded

The martagon lily and its hybrids are very easy to identify in the garden. They have many small flowers (1–2 inches across), all facing straight down. I am told that the common name Turk's-cap comes from the resemblance of each flower to . . . well, a Turk's cap. Each petal is curled well back away from the central reproductive organs, a form that botanists call "recurved." Although most lily petals open straight out or form a trumpet, the flowers of this class curve right back almost against themselves. The long stamen (the parts with the pollen) hang well down outside the flower petals, and the pollen itself is yellow. It is not unusual to have 40 flowers on each 4-foot-tall stem. The martagon class is fragrant, although the perfume is not as powerful as that of the other classes. They are quite resistant to viral diseases but are bothered by fungus. Plant them where they will receive good air movement and sunshine to reduce this problems.

Asiatic Lilies

Height: 3–4 feet

Bloom time: Third week of June to third week of July in zone 4

Depth to Plant: 4 to 6 inches

Spacing: 6–8 inches

Best Season to Plant: Early fall

Sunlight Needed: Leaves in full sun; bulb shaded

Lilium 'Enchantment' (Asiatic)

The Asiatic class of lilies is a mixed bag of breeding and flower forms. Gardeners should pay close attention to the catalog descriptions, because flower and color vary widely. The Asiatics are characterized by a midsized open-style bloom without much trumpet depth and slightly recurved petals, placing them somewhere between the trumpet and martagon classes. They are heavy-blooming plants. Their sturdy 3–4-foot-tall stems remain upright in most weather conditions, making them fine for the middle of the perennial border. Asiatic lilies are available in a wide range of colors, and the fragrance is minimal to nonexistent. These bulbs are quite popular because of their low cost, resistance to disease, and abundant blooms. Asiatic lilies are perfect for those of us who require lots of bulbs and color in the early summer garden. This is an excellent class of lilies for naturalizing or planting in rough, noncultivated areas.

easy fall bloomers

The Essentials

- Plant Portraits for Easy Fall Bloomers

Fall-blooming bulbs are wonderful when they are happy in their garden location. Unfortunately for those of us gardening in northern areas, they tend to be more tender than their spring-blooming cousins; so some of the plants listed here will simply not do well in areas colder than zone 5 or 6. Also, these bulbs are usually small plants, not suited for the perennial border but excellent for the rock garden. To get fall-blooming bulbs in colder areas, manipulate the planting dates of summer-flowering plants such as gladiolus (page 107).

Plant Portraits for Easy Fall Bloomers

Arum italicum

Height: 12 inches for foliage; 14 inches for flower stem
Bloom time: May; fall foliage in zone 6
Depth to Plant: 5 inches
Spacing: 6–8 inches
Best Season to Plant: Fall
Sunlight needed: Full sun or part shade

Arum is an easy and interesting addition to gardens located in areas no colder than zone 6. Although the flowers are not spectacular, the foliage is wonderful in the fall garden. In late summer, the plant develops distinctive silver-yellow veined patterns on its luscious dark green leaves. The foliage lasts all winter, going dormant early the following summer. The flowers are inconspicuous compared to other bulbs,

Arum italicum

but arum produces showy orange-red berries. Note that the berries can be used medicinally if prepared properly; however, they can be poisonous if eaten raw and in large quantities. Old medicinal books, called herbals, recommend consuming a single drachma of arum preparation every morning for gout, rheumatism, scurvy, palsy, and loss of appetite. Modern gardeners, having no clue what a drachma is, simply admire arum for its beauty.

The bulbs are normally available in the fall during fall bulb sales. Fall planting gives them an opportunity to set roots in preparation for the next season's growth. The first time I planted them, they did not come up in the spring; and not having read anything about them before I planted them, I assumed they were dead. (Writing these lines, I am reminded of a family saying: Do as I say, not as I do. It *is* helpful to know the plant's needs and habits *before* planting.) I did follow the label instructions, planting them 5 inches deep in a good, rich, and well-drained soil where they would be dry all summer but be appropriately damp for the fall and spring growing seasons. A small knoll in my side bulb bed was the perfect spot, high enough to dry out in the summer and protected from the worst of the winter winds by a being tucked up against a large boulder. When the arum did not appear that spring, I assumed the worst and forgot them. The silly things then stuck their heads up in mid-August and gave me a real show of wonderful foliage. I never did see them that winter in my zone 4 garden, as the snow buried them 4 feet deep. By the following spring they were quite dead, well frozen in place.

The second time I planted arum, I ensured they had a protected spot with perhaps a bit more shade and better soil. Again, they did not appear in the spring, but this time I was prepared. Their leaves came at the same time as the frost that year, resulting in a short show of partially unfolded leaves. I suspect something ate them during the winter, because I never saw them again. I do have a policy of trying most things three times before declaring my inability to grow them. This gives me another chance at arum; and I am waiting until I landscape the back of our stone house, so I can give it the warmest possible garden site available—the south side of a heated stone wall. Until then, I will have to believe the books that say the hardiest of arums will take a 14°F frost and no more.

This hardiest arum is *A. italicum,* which is the plant for a garden in zone 6 or warmer. Gardeners in zone 5 could pick the warmest spot in the garden and try one or two bulbs. *A. italicum* is the main plant grown for consumer sales; whereas the other arum species are normally available only through specialist plant societies or specialist growers. Other species are more tender.

If you are unable to grow arum outside, you'll be quite successful growing it in a cool greenhouse or on a windowsill for the winter and then plunging the pot outside for the summer. Plunging means burying the pot in the garden to just below the rim. I leave the rim exposed, which helps me find them in the fall. When the weather cools in the fall, dig up the pot and move it to its warmer winter resting place. See "Pots" on page 134 for more information.

As I mentioned, the orange-red berries are well worth seeing on their long stalk; they are nice in cut flower arrangements and can be dried. The spring flowers are no competition for a tulip or daffodil in color or impact; but they have interesting shapes and will encourage garden conversations

IS AN ARUM BY ANY OTHER NAME STILL AN ARUM?

In the literature on arums, there is some confusion between just what is an *A. italicum*. Plants sold under the name *A. italicum* 'Pictum', *A. italicum* 'Marmoratum', and *A. marmoratum* are quite likely to be the same plant, although originally bred from different clones. Also understand that *A. marmoratum* is a name of no known horticultural value. Plants sold under this name are likely either the *A. italicum* or *A. cocinnatum*. Taxonomists are still debating the terminology of the *Arum* genus. Please note that *A. italicum* 'Pictum' is hardier and different from *A. pictum*. *A. pictum* is sometimes offered in garden catalogs, but it will tolerate only a degree or two of frost. This makes it an ideal candidate for potting and plunging.

Whatever the name, a cultivation hint that may make a difference is always to mix lime into the planting area and never to mix in peat moss when planting arums. Arums are most frequently found on calcareous soils (limestone-based, alkaline soils), so acidic peat moss is of little use to them. If your soil requires organic matter, use compost instead of peat. The compost, if completely done, will have a neutral pH (neither acid nor alkaline).

and questions, mostly of the "What are those?" type. Some varieties and species have a bit of a fragrance to them, but you have to get close to the flowers to appreciate it. Grow arum for their foliage and winter interest.

Colchicum

Autumn Crocus, Naked Lady

Height: 4–6 inches

Bloom time: Fourth week of August to second week of September in zones 4–5

Depth to Plant: 4 inches

Spacing: 2–4 inches

Best Season to Plant: Fall

Sunlight needed: Full sun

Colchicum autumnale

Naked ladies are an interesting plant for the rock garden; and if they are happy in their location, they'll naturalize. *C. autumnale* is the hardiest of the genus and is reliably hardy down to –4°F, which translates into a gardening zone 5. I have had them winter over in my zone 4 garden but not regularly and only in the warmer parts of the garden. When they do survive, they are delightful with their rose-mauve blooms popping up when I least expect them. They flower and put their leaves up almost simultaneously; so if the season is short in colder gardens, they will not have enough time to gather energy for the next year's blooms and survival. Naked ladies love well-drained soils; if the soil is wet during the summer, the bulbs will likely rot away before they get a chance to bloom. *C. autumnale* will tolerate some shade in hotter gardens and is quite nice when allowed to naturalize underneath shrubs and trees.

Other species that are sometimes available for warmer gardens include *C. byzantinum,* which sports large purplish pink blossoms and is hardy into zone 6; and *C. speciosum,* which has large amethyst flowers, is 8 inches tall, and is hardy into zone 5.

Crocus

Crocus

Fall-blooming crocus are more tender than their spring-blooming cousins, and I have indicated this in each plant portrait. Personal experience says that if the fall-blooming crocus are planted in areas colder than their recommended gardening zone, they seldom survive. This is a shame but, unfortunately, a gardening fact of life for those of us who live in northern gardening areas. As a rule of thumb, these crocus do well in areas that receive summer rainfalls; they do not require a dry, dormant period during the summer months. They will also benefit from some light shade in areas of high summer heat. Plant them at a depth of 2 inches in the fall, when they are commonly available in catalogs and garden centers.

C. kotschyanus

Height: 5 inches
Bloom time: Fourth week of August in zone 6
Depth to Plant: 2 inches
Spacing: 2–3 inches
Best Season to Plant: Fall
Sunlight needed: Full sun to part shade

C. kotschyanus won the General Merit Award from the British Royal Horticultural Society, which indicates it is an excellent garden performer. Unfortunately, it is not likely to survive, let alone perform, north of zone 6. Zone 6 gardeners will experience the fall glory of this plant. Put its pinkish violet blossoms in rock gardens or other areas where there is no competition for the 5-inch-tall blossoms.

C. sativus

Height: 5 inches

Bloom time: Fourth week of August in zone 6

Depth to Plant: 2 inches

Spacing: 2–3 inches

Best Season to Plant: Fall

Sunlight needed: Full sun to part shade

Crocus sativus

C. sativus is the original source of saffron. Hardy into warmer zone 5 gardens, it has a beautiful lilac blossom that is well suited for the autumn rock garden. As a botanical note, this plant is a sterile form of *C. cartwrightianus,* a bulb native to Greece and slightly more tender than *C. sativus. C. cartwrightianus* is sometimes found in specialist catalogs and can be planted in warmer zone 7 gardens. The enterprising gardener can collect the pollen (saffron) from the *C. sativus* flowers, but it takes an incredible number of flowers to produce a useable amount of the spice; saffron is currently selling for $100 an ounce.

C. speciosus

Height: 5 inches

Bloom time: Fourth week of August in zone 6

Depth to Plant: 2 inches

Spacing: 2–3 inches

Best Season to Plant: Fall

Sunlight needed: Full sun to part shade

Crocus speciosus

Colder-zone gardeners would do well to stick to *C. speciosus,* as it is hardy into zone 4 gardens. Native to northern Turkey, it is quite lovely in the rock garden at the end of August. The colors of this species and its hybrids range from white through violets and blues. The color of the blooms does not really matter, because you will never meet one of these crocus you do not like.

Nerine Bowdenii

Height: 24 inches

Bloom time: September to October in zone 7

Depth to Plant: 1–2 inches

Spacing: 6 inches

Best Season to Plant: Fall

Sunlight needed: Full sun

Nerine bowdenii

Unfortunately, there is only one species of *Nerine,* gorgeous fall-blooming bulbs, that is at all frost hardy. *N. bowdenii* has rose-pink flowers and is hardy to zone 7. The rest of the genus must be grown in areas where frost does not visit. These bulbs demand good drainage and summer dryness for their dormancy period and will rot if these conditions are not met. Many gardeners, even in warmer areas, grow nerine in pots, to protect them from frost and to control their water requirements. This bulb will produce abundant flowers once it is potbound. If you are a beginner gardener, by all means try this bulb, but nerine is not commonly available or all that easily conquered.

forcing bulbs

for year-round enjoyment

The Essentials

- Preferred Conditions for Optimum Blooms
- Summer and Winter Plunging Tips
- Planting the Bulbs
- Forcing the Bulbs
- What to Do with Gift Bulbs

With the right kind of care, any bulb can be grown in a pot and forced into bloom. When I use the term *forcing,* I mean bringing a plant into flower or leaf sooner than it normally would if left outdoors.

Preferred Conditions for Optimum Blooms

The secret producing optimum blooms is to give the bulb the conditions it likes; if it gets its preferred conditions, you get the blooms. Most of these conditions involve very simple things, such as the water, temperature, and length of dormancy. The conditions for the most commonly forced bulbs are described below.

Soils

The first secret to growing good potted bulbs is to use the right soil. Use a well-draining potting soil available from most garden shops. Many indoor bulb enthusiasts swear by very free draining cactus-type mixes. You apply water when it is needed, but this potting mix allows the bulb to be dry during its dormancy period. As a rule of thumb, if the bulb is to be kept in the pot for more than one growing season, use a cactus or sandy mix. If you plan to keep the bulbs potted up for only one or two months and then either plant them outside or discard them, use either regular potting soil or a soilless mix. If in doubt, use a good potting soil.

Pots

If you have ever forced bulbs or grown houseplants, then you probably have very definite ideas about the kind of pot that does best under your house's growing conditions. I have grown plants in both clay and plastic and each has advantages and disadvantages. To begin with, I confess clay appeals to my sense of aesthetics more than plastic, and it looks much better on my kitchen windowsill. Clay is also heavier and counterbalances the considerable weight of taller bulbs, such as amaryllis, much better than plastic does. Clay dries out quicker than plastic, though; so if you tend to underwater your plants, you will have more problems with clay than with plastic. Clay is breakable, and nothing hurts the pocketbook and gardening frame of mind more than seeing a plunged clay pot shatter under the pressure of freezing or hard knocks. To its advantage, clay is cooler in the summer than plastic, because of the evaporative cooling from the sides of the pot.

Each will grow a good forced bulb. If you follow the finger test for watering, described below, then appropriate amounts of water will be applied and the pot choice becomes a matter of style or, often, which type is in the garage ready to use.

Watering Indoors

The finger test will keep beginning gardeners out of trouble caused by applying too much or too little water for their bulbs. If in doubt about whether to water, keep in mind the following guidelines. If you put your finger on the potted bulb soil and it comes away damp, then no water is needed. The soil has enough water; and no matter whether it has been one hour or one month since the last watering, if your finger is damp after touching the soil, the plant is fine. When the soil feels wet to the touch but there is no moisture on your finger, there is still enough water in the soil for the average bulb during its growing season. When your finger touches dry soil, then and only then can watering be done. Soil that is just dry to the touch usually has residual water farther down in the pot, but the water can stand to be replenished during the growing season when the plant is using it—especially if the plant is in the sun. If you're ever in doubt about watering, wait a few hours or until the next day and give the pot the finger test again. Always water so that 15 percent of the water runs through to the saucer underneath the pot; be sure to empty the saucer so the pot does not stand in water.

If the bulbs are to be saved after forcing or if the pot is to be plunged in the garden, continue this watering method until the foliage of the bulb has faded or until after the last spring frost, when the pot can be put outside. Weekly applications of liquid plant food, preferably a low-nitrogen, high-potash formula will replenish the bulb's stores. Apply this from blooming time until the foliage fades. When the foliage starts to fade, the bulb is ready for its dormant period. Refer to the appropriate plant portrait in Parts Three to Five to learn how much moisture the bulb needs during dormancy.

Temperature

Bulbs require a dormancy period, and most of the commonly forced bulbs, such as narcissus, tulips, and hyacinth, require a cold dormancy before they are able to bloom. For the flower bud to properly form, tulips must—absolutely must—have a cold dormancy period of twelve to fifteen weeks during which the temperature is 41 to 48°F. In nature, this occurs in the late fall, when soil temperatures drop for the cool seasons. In the home, there are several ways to achieve the same effect. The first is to purchase precooled bulbs that have already gone through the dormancy period. These are labeled by retailers as "precooled" or "prechilled" bulbs suitable for forcing. Simply pot these up, follow the directions below for temperature and light, and enjoy their blooms. The second method is to chill the bulbs yourself. The easiest way to do this is to plant the bulbs in pots and plunge them in the garden where the cool outdoor temperatures will meet the dormancy needs of the bulbs. Once they have had their twelve to fifteen weeks of chilling, bring them back indoors two to three weeks before you want flowers.

The bulbs can also be put in the refrigerator crisper for the fifteen weeks of cooling. There are several drawbacks to this system that must be attended to. The first is to never store your bulbs along with ripening vegetables or fruit. The ethylene gas given off by the ripening food damages the flower potential of many bulbs. Second, a constant check must be kept on the bulbs to ensure they are not developing mold because of a liquid spill or too high humidity. A third concern is small children or ravenous teenagers eating the bulbs. Some bulbs are poisonous and should not be kept loose if small children are in the habit of raiding the fridge. If these three concerns are met, the crisper will do as good a job of bulb storage as any professional cooler. If kept in the refrigerator, the bulbs will not have a chance to set roots, unlike bulbs plunged in the garden; so it will take some extra time before they will set flowers when returned to growing conditions.

Summer and Winter Plunging Tips

Plunging is an excellent, low-maintenance method of keeping bulbs alive for the summer months with minimal work. I plunge most of my stock plants and houseplants outside during the summer, both for their health and for my ease of watering and care. Plunging means placing the pot into the soil with only the rim showing. For summer dormancy bulbs, put the pot under the eaves of a building where water will seldom penetrate. For bulbs that require water during the summer, such as amaryllis, put them in the regular flower or vegetable garden, where they will obtain rainfall and watering-can attention. In the fall, you can insulate hardy bulbs where they sit with several feet of leaves or dry peat moss. *Dry* peat moss is an excellent protective material, because it does not freeze solid, so you'll be able to dig through it to obtain the pots for forcing. Never use wet peat moss, as it turns into a block of solid ice and is impossible to move or dig through without a great deal of effort. Leaves also work very well, particularly if they can be kept dry before freezing temperatures arrive.

Some gardeners bury their pots in 12-inch-deep trenches and backfill the trenches with peat moss, leaves, or straw. Some even use cold frames that can be opened up to regularly sneak a pot or two of the bulbs for the house. The objective is to cool the potted bulbs but not allow them to freeze. It is difficult to move frozen pots and bulbs without ruining them.

If the pots are well protected, they can be dug out anytime you feel the need for flowers. As a rule of thumb, twenty-one days after digging up a pot from the ground, flowers will start to form for most garden species. Smaller, earlier bulbs are a few days faster than taller, later bulbs.

Planting the Bulbs

The best planting advice for beginners is to do two things when forcing bulbs. The first is not to mix different types of bulbs in the same planter. Different bulbs have different rooting and flowering schedules, and until you have spent some time experimenting with your growing conditions to make sure you can bring them all into bloom at the same time, the odds are that you will be disappointed in the results. It is much better to plant like bulbs in each pot and then put the pots together in one location. The second piece of advice is to crowd the bulbs in the pot. A truly great show of potted bulbs will come only if there are loads of flowers in the pot. A few potted flowers look very lonely blooming out of season.

Planting is quite simple. The flowerpot can be as wide as desired, but the depth for bulbs is usually in the 6-inch range. I use azalea-style pots, which are shorter than the standard pots. Put 2 inches of soil in the bottom of the pot, and place the bulbs on the soil. Do not ram them into the soil, crushing the bulb; instead, gently fill the pot with bulbs, getting them as close as possible without bruising. Add enough soil to fill the pot, tucking the soil around the bulbs; then water the pot with lukewarm water to settle the soil.

You might want to experiment with one pot of double-decker bulbs. Use a taller pot, at least 8 inches high; plant the first layer of bulbs, and cover them with soil. Water these bulbs in so the soil settles, top the damp soil with 1 inch of level soil, and plant another layer of bulbs. Fill in with more soil, and water. The pot is now crammed full of bulbs and will give a monstrous display of flowers when it blooms.

Forcing the Blooms

When the bulbs are moved from their storage area into the warmth, they immediately begin to grow. This initial growth stage is best done in medium sunshine and with a room temperatures of 60°F. For practical purposes, a good sunny south window during the winter will be excellent, and the temperature of 60°F is ideal but not critical. When the shoots are approximately 6 inches tall, the plants require as much light as possible and a slightly higher temperature to stimulate the flowering response. This is the time to give them the south-facing window and 68 to 70°F room temperatures. The flower buds grow best at this higher temperature; and this is, after all, what we are trying to achieve. Once the flower buds start to show color, they can be either left where they are in a sunny spot or moved to a sunny, well-lit spot with indirect sunlight. If the pot is left in the very sunny location, the flower life may be a day or two shorter than if the pot were moved to the indirect but well-lit spot.

When choosing between two places to force bulbs, always pick the one with the higher light level. Lots of light is more important than temperature for ensuring the plants do not stretch and flop over.

If you are trying to have blooms for a specific date, higher temperatures will speed up the process and cooler room temperatures will slow the growth. If the twenty-one-day rule of thumb is kept in mind, then starting the forcing process twenty-five to twenty-eight days before a special event will almost guarantee a good show of color. Get the bloom into color a few days before the event, and then cool it down until the morning of the event. The morning of the event, place the bulbs where they are to be seen; and they will quickly start to develop in the higher heat.

Which Bulbs Can Be Forced?

Instead of asking which bulbs can be forced, ask which bulbs *cannot* be forced. The two easiest and most common bulbs for forcing are the amaryllis and paper-white narcissus. Large-flowering crocus are very easy, as are anemone, daffodils, hyacinth, tulips, grape hyacinth, and bulbous iris. In well-draining soil, almost any bulb that can be purchased in the fall can be forced during the long, bloom-deprived winter days by following the easy directions described here or by purchasing precooled bulbs at your favorite garden retailer.

Amaryllis

Gardeners in the south (zones 9 and 10) can grow amaryllis as an outdoor bulb, but the rest of us treat it as an indoor, frost-tender flower. When choosing a bulb, there is only one rule: Bigger is better. If the bulb is hard to the touch, and the flower color is to your liking, the bigger the bulb, the better the chances of having two flower stems and up to eight blooms the first year.

To obtain good blooms, use a good-quality potting soil and plant the bulb in a 6-inch pot. One-third of the bulb should be aboveground, and the initial watering should be with lukewarm water. Use the finger test, and keep the soil damp but not soggy or the bulb will rot. To encourage flowering the temperature should be 70 to 75°F until the flower stalks begin to grow. Once

Amaryllis hippeastrum

the amaryllis stalks begin to shoot up, the plant prefers a temperature 10° cooler. Put the pot in full sunlight until the blossoms begin to show color; then move it to indirect lighting, because the blooms fade quickly in full sunlight. Amaryllis is one bulb that does tend to grow toward the light. To avoid "leaning towers of amaryllis," rotate the pot ninety degrees every day to equalize the light exposure.

Getting an amaryllis to flower again involves only a few simple rules. One rule is to water and feed the bulb as a houseplant after flowering. They have only one bloom period a year, so the straplike leaves will require regular weekly feeding with houseplant food to keep them growing and renewing the flower-producing energy. Many gardeners plunge the pot in the garden for the summer. After summer, the key ingredient in the recipe is to make sure the bulb gets an eight- to ten-week, late fall storage period at a temperature of 45 to 55°F. The flower bud sets during this cool dormancy. Some gardeners pop the bulb out of the pot during dormancy and allow the bulb to dry out in its cool period. Don't water a potted bulb during this time; allow the bulb to go fully dormant and dry. Once the bulb has passed the ten-week mark, the bulb can be left until it naturally starts to send up a shoot, or it can be brought up into the light and forced into bloom again.

Bulbs that are several years old often develop baby offshoot bulbs beside the main bulb. These can be left on the old bulb to develop and produce more flower shoots, or you can carefully separate them and pot them up on their own. If the mother bulb and still-attached babies are put into a slightly larger pot (generally move plants up 1 inch in pot size with every repotting) a real flower show can be seen when the babies start producing their own flowers.

Paper-White Narcissus

Paper-whites are a favorite of winter bulb growers, because they do not require a twelve-week rooting or dormancy period. Easily available in many retail locations during the winter months, they are perfect plants for beginners. Pot them up and leave them in a cool area without a great deal of light. The roots will take three weeks to develop; then move the pot into a sunny area for forcing. They do best in a gravel soil. If gravel is unavailable, aquarium gravel works well; wash it well to remove any salt that might contaminate the bulbs, and put 2 inches of gravel on the bottom of the pot. Cover the bulbs with the remaining gravel to keep these little beauties quite happy. If gravel is not available, then sand will substitute nicely, as will cactus-type soils. Water regularly, but do not let paper-white bulbs sit in waterlogged soil or gravel mixes. If gravel is used, then set the potted bulbs onto a small saucer of water. The gravel will slowly wick the required moisture up to the bulb roots, and there will be no danger of overwatering or underwatering.

Some paper-whites come with a glass or clear plastic growing vase. The bulbs can be grown in clear water if the water line is kept at the basal plate of the bulb but no higher.

Two last thoughts on paper-whites need to be passed along to beginners. The first is to consider purchasing a large supply of paper-whites whenever they are available in the stores. Plant a few containers every two weeks to get an almost continuous succession of blooms throughout the winter months; store the rest in the refrigerator crisper. The second is that paper-whites have a distinctive fragrance that gardeners either enjoy or detest. There is little middle ground—you either like it or hate it. I do not grow paper-whites indoors.

Narcissus tazetta

PROGRAM FOR YEAR-ROUND BULB ENJOYMENT

Bulbs are meant to be enjoyed; and with a little planning and forethought,
they can give flowering pleasure all year.

Month	To Do
January	Plant paper-whites every two weeks; bring in a pot of dormant bulbs, one every two weeks for continuous blooms
February	Continue as above for blooms
March	Continue as above; in warmer zones look for first spring bloomers
April	Spring-blooming bulbs are well under way in most garden zones
May	Tulips and other spring bloomers are at their height; begin planting summer bloomers; deadhead spring bloomers
June	Continue succession planting of summer bloomers; enjoy late spring bloomers; continue deadheading and cleaning up spring bloomers
July	Enjoy early summer bloomers, including lilies; routine maintenance of flowers
August	Enjoy summer bloomers, including lilies; begin deadheading lilies; continue routine maintenance; drool over fall bulb catalogs, ordering at least one new and different bulb every year
September	Enjoy late summer bloomers and fall bloomers; harvest buds with color before killing frost; plant fall tulips and spring bulbs in zone 3 in late September; pot up and plunge first batch of bulbs for early indoor harvest
October	Enjoy late-harvested summer blossoms; enjoy fall bloomers at their peak; plant spring bulbs and fall lilies in most gardening zones; pot up spring bulbs for spring forcing
November	Start bringing in pots of forced bulbs to enjoy
December	Bring in pots of spring bulbs to force; enjoy Christmas blooms and florist-forced plants

What to Do with Gift Bulbs

Be sure to plant up any gift bulbs you might receive. If the gift is an unpotted bulb, then handle it as suggested earlier in this section. If the bulb has already been potted up by a florist, grow it according to the directions given in this part. Once blooming has finished, start growing the foliage. This means giving the bulb weekly feedings of a low-nitrogen, high-potash liquid houseplant food and full sunshine. Normal room temperatures are perfect for this growth period. Allow the soil to dry to the touch between waterings, but don't let the pot fully dry out. Use the finger test method described in "Watering Indoors" on page 135. When all danger of spring frost has passed in your area, plant the bulb outside as you would any other spring plant, following the directions given in that bulb's plant portrait (Parts Three to Five). Most bulbs readily accept being moved after they've bloomed and while their leaves are still green. Relax and allow nature to take its course for the following spring.

Bulb Sources

United States Mail-Order Bulb Suppliers

JACQUES AMAND
Potomac, MD
800-452-5414

Full assortment of bulbs

VERNON BARNES & SON NURSERY
McMinnville, TN
615-668-8576

Assortment of bulbs

ANTONELLI BROTHERS
Santa Cruz, CA
408-475-5222

Begonias, ranunculus, dahlias,
gladiolus, lilies

B&D LILIES
Port Townsend, WA
360-385-1738

Full assortment of lilies and daylilies

BORBELETA GARDENS, INC.

Fairbault, MN

507-334-2807

Assortment of bulbs

BRECK'S DUTCH BULBS

Peoria, IL

800-722-9069

Full assortment of bulbs

BUNDLES OF BULBS

Owings Mills, MD

410-581-2188

Assortment of bulbs

BURGESS SEED & PLANT CO.

Bloomington, IL

309-663-9551

Assortment of bulbs

W. ALTEE BURPEE, & CO.

Warminister, PA

800-888-1447

Full assortment of bulbs

COOLEY'S GARDENS, INC.

Silverton, OR

800-225-5391

Bearded iris

DAFFODIL MART

Gloucester, VA

800-255-2852

Full assortment of bulbs

DUTCH GARDENS

Adelphia, NJ

800-818-3861

Full assortment of bulbs

FERRY-MORSE SEEDS

Fulton, KY

800-283-3400

Assortment of bulbs

HENRY FIELD SEED & NURSERY CO.

Shenandoah, IA

605-665-4491

Full assortment of bulbs

FRENCH'S

Pittsfield, VT

800-286-8198

Selection of fall-planted bulbs

GEERLINGS BULBS USA

Babylon, NY

www.dutchflowers.com

Online source of Dutch bulbs

RUSSELL GRAHAM PURVEYOR OF PLANTS

Salem, OR

503-362-1135

Assortment of bulbs

GURNEY SEED

Yankton, SD

605-665-9310

Full assortment of bulbs

HARRIS SEEDS

Rochester, NY

800-514-4441

Full assortment of bulbs

JACKSON & PERKINS

Medford, OR

800-854-6200

Full assortment of bulbs

J. W. JUNG SEED CO.

Randolph, WI

800-247-5864

Full assortment of bulbs

KLEHM NURSERY

South Barrington, IL

800-553-3715

Iris and other bulbs

McCLURE & ZIMMERMAN

Friesland, WI

414-326-4220

Full assortment of bulbs

MICHIGAN BULB CO.

Grand Rapids, MI

616-735-2100

Full assortment of bulbs

CHARLES H. MUELLER CO.

New Hope, PA

215-862-2033

Full assortment of bulbs

NETHERLAND BULB CO.

Easton, PA

800-755-2852

Full assortment of bulbs

OLD HOUSE GARDENS

Ann Arbor, MI

313-995-1486

Antique bulbs; heritage bulbs

GEO. W. PARK SEED CO.

Greenwood, SC

800-845-3369

Full assortment of flower bulbs

ROBINETT BULB FARM
Sebastopol, CA
707-829-2729

Specialty bulbs, including
California natives

RORIS GARDENS
Sacramento, CA
916-689-7460

Tall bearded iris specialists

JOHN SCHEEPERS
Bantam, CT
860-567-0838

Full assortment of bulbs

SCHIPPER & CO.
Greenwich, CT
203-625-0638

Colorblend collections of bulbs

SCHREINER'S IRIS GARDENS
Salem, OR
800-525-2367

Bearded iris specialists

SPRING HILL NURSERIES
Peoria, IL
800-544-0294

Full assortment of bulbs

TERRITORIAL SEED CO.
Cottage Grove, OR
541-942-9547

Fall-planted bulbs

**THOMAS JEFFERSON CENTER
FOR HISTORIC PLANTS**
Monticello, Charlottesville, VA
804-984-9819

Selected plants and flower
bulbs known to have been
grown by Thomas Jefferson.

THOMPSON & MORGAN
Jackson, NJ
800-274-7333

Assortment of bulbs

VAN BOURGONDIEN BROS.
Babylon, NY
800-622-9997

Full assortment of bulbs

VAN DYCK'S FLOWER FARMS
Brightwaters, NY
800-248-2852

Full assortment of bulbs

WAYSIDE GARDENS
Hodges, SC
800-845-1124

Full assortment of bulbs

VAN ENGELEN
Litchfield, CT
860-567-8734

Full assortment of bulbs

WHITE FLOWER FARM
Litchfield, CT
800-503-9624

Full assortment of bulbs

VELDHEER TULIP GARDENS
Holland, MI
616-399-1900

Full assortment of bulbs

Canadian Mail-Order Bulb Suppliers

AIMERS
Aurora, Ontario
416-841-6226

Full assortment of bulbs

DOMINION SEED HOUSE
Georgetown, Ontario
905-873-3037

Full assortment of bulbs

CRUICKSHANK LTD.
Toronto, Ontario
416-488-8292

Full assortment of bulbs

GARDENIMPORT INC.
Thornhill, Ontario
905-731-1950

Full assortment of bulbs

HORTICLUB

Laval, Quebec

514-682-9071

Full assortment of bulbs

McCONNELL & McFAYDEN SEED CO.

Brandon, Manitoba

800-205-7111

Full assortment of bulbs

Other

NETHERLANDS FLOWER BULB INFORMATION CENTER

www.bulb.com

An excellent on-line source of information, including growing tips, data, photos, mail-order sources, and much more

USDA Plant Hardiness Zone Map

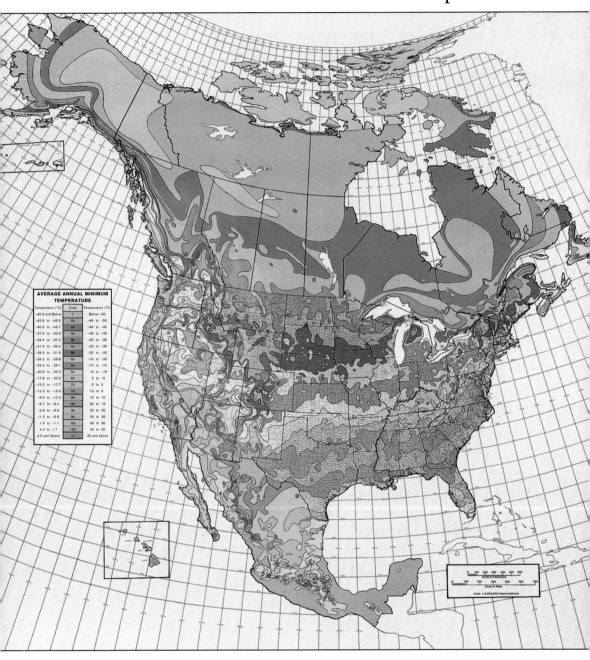

AVERAGE ANNUAL MINIMUM TEMPERATURE		
Temperature (°C)	Zone	Temperature (°C)
-45.6 and Below	1	Below -50
-42.8 to -45.5	2a	-45 to -50
-40.0 to -42.7	2b	-40 to -45
-37.3 to -40.0	3a	-35 to -40
-34.5 to -37.2	3b	-30 to -35
-31.0 to -34.4	4a	-25 to -30
-28.9 to -31.6	4b	-20 to -25
-26.2 to -28.8	5a	-15 to -20
-23.4 to -26.1	5b	-10 to -15
-20.6 to -23.3	6a	-5 to -10
-17.8 to -20.5	6b	0 to -5
-15.0 to -17.7	7a	5 to 0
-12.3 to -15.0	7b	10 to 5
-9.5 to -12.2	8a	15 to 10
-6.7 to -9.4	8b	20 to 15
-3.9 to -6.6	9a	25 to 20
-1.2 to -3.8	9b	30 to 25
1.6 to -1.1	10a	35 to 30
4.4 to 1.7	10b	40 to 35
4.5 and Above	11	40 and above

The Gardener's Language

Acid soil: see *pH*.

Alkaline soil: see *pH*.

Annual: A plant that lasts for only one season in the garden and is killed by frost or freezing. In warmer climates it grows too large and must be drastically pruned or replanted from seed.

Balanced plant food: A fertilizer mix that contains equal amounts of nitrogen, phosphate, and potash. The following mixes are balanced: 7–7–7 and 15–15–15. A balanced mix is not necessarily the correct formula for a particular plant.

Bone meal: Bones processed and dried to a white powder. Used as a source of natural phosphorus in the garden.

Bulb: Belowground, modified leaf bud with fleshy scales or leaf bases that acts as an energy and food storage organ for the plant.

Compost: The initial product of plant or organic matter decomposition. Something gardeners should use in all areas of their gardens.

Corm: Belowground storage organ that is botanically part of the stem, not the leaf.

Cultivar: A plant that has been bred to be slightly different from and, it is hoped, improved over the original wild plant. Cultivars are maintained in the garden setting.

Deciduous: Trees and shrubs that lose their leaves in the fall.

Deep planting: Planting bulbs deeper than normally recommended. Used as a rodent control.

Dormancy: The time when a plant is not vigorously growing but resting. Normally during the winter months.

Drip line: The circumference around a tree or shrub that is defined by the reach of the plant's limbs or foliage.

Forcing: Causing a plant to bloom or grow during a time when it is normally dormant.

Garden or hardiness zone: A number assigned to a general geographic division, defined by average minimum and maximum temperatures, that can be used to determine which plants will or will not grow in that particular area. The most commonly used system is the USDA Hardiness Zone Map, which divides the United States and Canada into ten zones. Rankings should be used as guidelines only.

Hardy or hardiness: A plant's ability to withstand cold temperatures.

Heavy soil: A soil that has a high clay content.

Horticultural Latin: The language of plant scientists. Allows gardeners on opposite sides of the world to be sure that they are discussing the same plant. It has a working place in horticulture and is a different language than "regular" Latin.

Humus: The final product of decomposing organic matter. Organic matter breaks down into compost, and compost breaks down into humus.

Hybrid: A plant grown from two parents that are genetically dissimilar.

Liquid plant food: A fertilizer that comes in a liquid form.

Mudding in: Slowly applying copious amounts of water to a just-planted garden area. Often used as a rodent deterrent.

Mulch: A layer of material, normally organic, placed on top of the soil to preserve water, reduce weed seed germination, and enhance the garden appearance.

Naturalizing: Planting bulbs and allowing them grow wild, self-sowing, spreading or not, as the natural environment determines.

Neutral soil: see *pH*.

Nitrogen: One of the three main nutrients needed for plant growth. Generally responsible for leaf growth and overall health of the plant.

Organic soil: Soil formed mainly from plant residues.

Overplanting: Adding plants above established bulbs so two crops of flowers can be obtained from the same garden area in a single year.

Perennial: A plant that should live for at least three years before dying. Some perennials are short lived, others very long lived.

pH: The measure of a soil's acidity, rated on a scale from 1 to 14, with 1 being highly acid and 14 being highly alkaline. Soils with a pH value of 7 are neutral.

Phosphorus: One of the "big three" nutrients needed by plants for growth. It generally assists root development. Note that it does not readily move through the soil and should be put directly at the root-growing area for best results.

Plunging: Sinking a planted flowerpot into the soil up to its rim.

Potassium: One of the principal nutrients needed for plant growth. It contributes to overall plant health and flower formation.

Rhizome: An underground stem that sends up leaves or new plant stems.

Tuber: An underground stem or branch that is usually thicker than the main stem. It serves as a storage organ, sending new shoots from buds, or eyes.

Tunic: A loose membrane around a bulb, not part of its skin.

Umbel: A flower form in which multiple smaller blossoms all have the same stem length and join together at a common point to form a larger blossom.

Variety: An official botanical subdivision of a species that ranks below the subspecies in a plant genus. Often used incorrectly as a synonym for *cultivar.*

Index

Page numbers in *italics* indicate photographs or illustrations.